Tying Knots

Step-by-step Guide to Knots Tying and Using

(Learn How to Tie and Identify Essential Knots for Sailing, Fishing, Climbing, and Camping)

Milton Crowder

Published By **Chris David**

Milton Crowder

Tying Knots: Step-by-step Guide to Knots Tying and Using (Learn How to Tie and Identify Essential Knots for Sailing, Fishing, Climbing, and Camping)

ISBN 978-1-9994868-4-6

No part of this guidebook shall be reproduced in any form without permission in writing from the publisher except in the case of brief quotations embodied in critical articles or reviews.

Legal & Disclaimer

The information contained in this book is not designed to replace or take the place of any form of medicine or professional medical advice. The information in this book has been provided for educational & entertainment purposes only.

The information contained in this book has been compiled from sources deemed reliable, and it is accurate to the best of the Author's knowledge; however, the Author cannot guarantee its accuracy and validity and cannot be held liable for any errors or omissions. Changes are periodically made to this book. You must consult your doctor or get professional medical advice before using any of the suggested remedies, techniques, or information in this book.

Upon using the information contained in this book, you agree to hold harmless the Author from and against any damages, costs, and expenses, including any legal fees potentially resulting from the application of any of the information provided by this guide. This disclaimer applies to any damages or injury caused by the use and application, whether directly or indirectly, of any advice or information presented, whether for breach of contract, tort, negligence, personal injury, criminal intent, or under any other cause of action.

You agree to accept all risks of using the information presented inside this book. You need to consult a professional medical practitioner in order to ensure you are both able and healthy enough to participate in this program.

Table Of Contents

Chapter 1: Knot Tying

If you consider the very first time you tied a knot, it is likely that you likely won't be in a position to identify exactly when it was. Knots are a constant part of our lives starting with the most basic of actions like tieing our shoes, to tying the tie, and tied hair ribbons. They can also be used for more intricate activities like tying the fishing line, or fastening the load.

It doesn't matter if you want to acknowledge it or you don't (no implied pun) knot-tying is a crucial skill to use in everyday life. It will require you to practice it occasionally.

Now let us look at an overview of the history behind knot-tying

Brief History of Knot Tying

As we look to the past, we find that the very earliest remains of knots and ropes can be traced from around 15,000 to 177,000 years back. This implies that the process of knots is much older than the wheel or axe. Knots have been around for a long time as an essential element in significant inventions including baskets as well as hunting traps. fishing nets.

How Were Knots Used in The Past?

Prior to trains, planes subways and automobiles were invented, transport was made by means of either animals or boats. It was essential to anchor the dock of the boats in order to prevent them from being dragged off by powerful waves. The animals also had to be bound to keep the animals from wandering off. In the time it was a simple task of tying a knot was a sign keeping something precious or the possibility of losing the item.

The most popular knot used to secure boats is known as the bowine knot. It was first used in the Egyptian period, based on fossils discovered from recently found vessels. As time it has been discovered that people can make hundreds of knots that vary from knots that are simple and are able to create in a matter of seconds to complex knots that need step-by-step instruction.

It has been demonstrated that this ability was extremely valuable back in the day, so why not we look at how important knot-tying is today in our society?

Here are the different methods we are currently using to apply this method:

Practical Applications of Knot Tying

Knot-tying is a good option in these situations:

1. Knots play a vital role in doing outdoor sports for example:

Mountaineering

Camping- e.g. creating some camping equipment and putting up tents

Hunting

Sailing/boating/seamanship/ canoeing

2. Knots are often used for crafts, but they are most commonly used when you make macrame. Macrame became a popular craft in the 1970s. The most well-known macrame knots are: the knot overhand, clove loop, spiral stitch square knot and Lark's Head Knot.

3. Truckers use the hitch of their truck to benefit from a mechanical advantage in securing their load.

4. This skill can be used to create tools that are improvised also; such as the munter hitch to use for making fasteners and in the bowline knot that is ideal as a safety loop.

5. It is also possible to tie knots to create an elevated line that is similar to a zip line. This could be used for moving injured persons, materials or even inexperienced individuals through crevices, ravines or down rivers.

Keep at heart that the techniques mentioned above typically require making use of various knots suitable for the task. correctly.

You may also use knots together to design intricate products like lanyards or netting.

Chapter 2: Knot Tying Terminology

Like many other skills in the technical field, once you begin to learn knot tying, it is likely that you'll encounter a variety of terminology that apply for this particular art. We have listed the most frequently used words to aid you in understanding this ability:

1. Standing Part and Running End

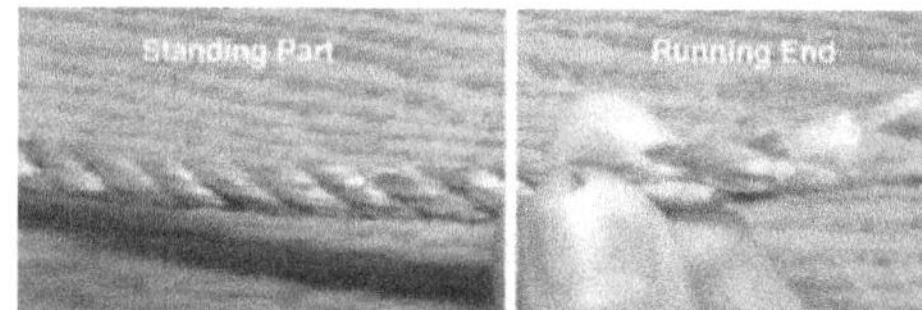

The working part is the portion of a cord engaged in knot tying -across to the part that is standing. Also known as the running or working component. However the standing end refers to the portion of cording that's not employed in knotting. It is also known as to the end that is used for work. The rope ends are lowered downwards to the landing spot or to the ground in case of abseiling or rappelling.

Be sure to secure a stopper knot at the same time as you are standing even though it could not touch the ground or even to the point of landing.

2. Bight

If you reverse an strand of cording back against itself, creating the U-shape you create an arc or a Bight. The bight can be created wherever you want across the standing area or even use the running portion. The length of bights could differ by a few feet up to several inches.

In the illustration below, on the right Bights are able to be opened, and don't need a sharp bent. The running part of the rope is, in this case is located next to the part that is standing, but it's not crossed (which could make it an overhand loop or underhand loop).

3. Take a Turn

It is the act of connecting a rope to the stake (or spar) for it to travel in a similar manner. It creates friction, which provides you with a grip on the stake, which helps to keep the tension on the line. This also gives you more control of removing and adding lines.

4. Round Turn

Round-turns are created by complete wrapping the rope around the stake before returning the running end over the stand part of the rope. It gives more control when it comes to maintaining tension of a rope. Round turns are the basis for creating many knots by using two half-hitches to make a circular turn.

5. Capsizing

If a knot changes shape to form a specific shape, it's considered to be capsized. Capsizing is often an consequence of improper or faulty knots, it is a method we employ to help strengthen knots when needed.

6. Dressing

The act of arranging the knot in a way which enhances the function of the knot is called knot dressing. The ability to improve the strength of your knot and reduce the chance of it to be jammed by removing or crossing the cord in a specific method, in accordance with the knot you chose to use.

7. Elbow

It is the term used to define the intersection of two points on rope that lie within close proximity. When you create an additional turn in the loop you make an elbow. This is the case when you tie butterflies knots.

8. Flake

A rope that is flaked will be coiled the rope. Flakes simply mean the number of turns on an uncoil rope.

9. Noose

The term "sliding loop" is commonly applied to describe an elastic loop that is tightened when you pull upon the loop.

10. Decorative Knot

Knot ties with decorative knots are among the oldest and most popular practiced by folk artists. This is simply an euphemism for any knot that looks pleasing. The majority of these knots originate from knots that are popular and may have practical uses in addition.

11. Hitch

It is a knot that can be that is used to attach an item to a cord such as a post rail, or spar.

12. Interlocking Elbow

If you bend two times around a rope in order to make two cross-points creating interlocking elbows. The interlocking elbow is typically used in knots, similar to those used by those of the Alpine Butterfly.

13. Friction Hitch

It is a knot which joins two cords to each other, in a manner that lets you adjust your knot's position quickly. It can be called the slide-and-grip knot. It is usually used for climbing. Examples of popular friction hitch knots are Prusik knot, and the rolling hitch.

14. Bend

This knot is made to attach two rope lengths.

15. Binding Knot

It is a knot which connects two objects or restricts one object. Seizings, lashings, and whippings knots - which are classified according to their type, and will be discussed in depth in the future book all serve the same purpose in the knot. But, they also contain numerous wraps which can be recognized as knots. If you are using binding knots, your cording's tails should be pulled beneath the turn of the knot or joined.

16. Jamming Knot

It is essentially knots that, after being tied, is extremely difficult to pull loose. However, the knots with no jams are ones that are invulnerable to jamming.

17. Loop Knot

It is a type of knot that forms an elongated loop which is then secured. It's formed in two situations: the moment a loop of the bight of your rope is tied or the end of the cord is tied by the point that is standing on that cord.

Contrary with a hitch knot is an unbreakable loop using an elastic cord which can keep its design regardless of whether it's attached to an object or it isn't. That means you are able to untie a loop knot on an object, but it'll keep its form.

18. Seizing

The knot of this kind joins two strands of cord in a row, typically to create loops. The structure likes the one used that is used for lashings.

19. Whipping

This kind of knot is tied on the cord's end to stop the cord from tearing.

20. Stopper Knot

The knot is used to secure an impermanent whipping, or to prevent the cord from sliding into grommet.

21. Slipped Knot

It is a knot that is unfastened when you release an end. Thus that when you tie a slip knot that is slipped, it's easier to loosen, especially when the knot is prone to getting jammed.

22. Splice

Connecting two ropes in which you twist and weave the rope strands is referred to as splicing rope.

23. Setting

The act of tightening knots is referred to as setting. Certain knots may not perform because of incorrect setting.

Chapter 3: Materials Required For Knot Tying

If you are looking to tie knots, the most important material you require is rope or cord, twine or any other materials that you can tie knots with.

Rope Selection: Rope for Practicing Knot Tying

You can make use of almost all ropes available online in a marine or hardware retailer to learn knot-tying.

Though you're able to utilize nearly all kinds of ropes, it's important to remember that not every kind of rope is a breeze to work with; some ropes are too slick or rigid or too stiff, while some are too expensive. Also, there isn't a single rope that's ideal for every knot.

A beer knot will require tubular webbing. A Brummel spice requires hollow braids, and the eye splice with 3 strands requires a three-strand twist rope.

As an aspiring beginner, here are some guidelines and suggestions that will help you choose an appropriate rope to learn the knots you are familiar with:

1. The Correct Rope and Size

Pick a rope which is not too shiny or slippery and also flexible. The strength is dependent on the job the rope is designed to be used.

The best fit is within the range 6-12mm (1/4" up to 1/4"). The size that falls within this range permits the knots be removed and the rope to be reused and allows for each knot to be seen clearly.

2. Ropes to Avoid

Beware of the polypropylene rope, which is typically sold in blue or yellow for towlines on water skis. These knots aren't able to hold securely, and the rope isn't safe to use.

Beware of the huge spools that contain 3 mm (1/8") twisting 3-strand nylon as well as the expensive modern string sold due to their unique design. It's safer to choose a thinner rope.

When we discuss the different kinds of ropes available, it's important to identify the most suitable fibers to use. Two main fibers are:

Natural Fibers

Natural fiber ropes will not lose knots and 3 stranded versions make them ideal to splice. Manila and the tarred hemp are both solid fiber ropes which can be used to learn how ways to knots. Manilla rope is made of manilla hemp which has been taken from the abaca leaves plant. Tarred hemp is hemp which has been coated with tar for protection of the fibers that are natural to it. Both of them hold their shape when spliced and make a stunning final splice.

However, this rope may not be available to you, specifically the size you want as it's expensive in addition to being federally unlawful.

Another challenge when dealing with ropes like these is that their ends aren't able to be burned to prevent fraying. You'll have be able to fix them using a knot, tape or constrictor or even make them whip.

Synthetic Fibers

The fiber-optic synthetic cord which is typically accessible is a nylon rope. Though you may make a seal on the raw end by with heat, you'll have to take extra care because any contact with the skin can cause a severe burning, and nylon is likely to melt when temperatures exceed 200 temperatures Celsius.

There are a variety of the traditional knots with nylon rope. The three-strand variant can be used for eye splice, a short splice and back splice. One of the main drawbacks to using the rope for splicing is that the fibers in each strand tend to be messy. This creates the appearance of an messy.

Additionally, clothesline rope has an outer coating of plastic that is extremely rigid and is suitable to knot.

For the braided cords that are sold at the marine market, that typically has an outer sheath as well as an inside core, it's excellent for teaching However, it's unnecessary costly as well.

There is also Polyethylene as well as polyester (Trevira(r), Terylene(r), Dacron(r)).

We now have the best kind of rope and which ones to stay clear of then we'll move on to talking about the effects knots can have on the strength of ropes:

Effect of Knots On Rope Strength

When it comes to knots and the strength of the rope is related to its ability to withstand the knot and the burden of the load. If you tie a knot your rope is weakened by the knot that you employ. The rope that is knotted usually fails close to the knot, or near the knot if you pull the rope to the point of breaking.

The crushing, restraining, and bending forces that are responsible to hold the knot in place will also result in an unbalanced tension on the fibers of the cord and ultimately reduces the strength. What can be done to maintain the power of rope, and to ensure it is as efficient as feasible?

Here are a few helpful suggestions:

It's essential to stretch (pull tightly) and then dress (make tidy) every knot before you use for ensuring that they won't unravel when you're working.

Please do not be able to walk or stand over the rope.

Do not drag the rope because abrasion may significantly affect the life of the sheath.

Don't disfigure or make the knot too tight.

Be sure to not leave your rope in tension for long periods of time.

Do not add types or twists in the process of coiling or bagging the rope.

Unfasten the knots one time throughout with the ropework.

Do not leave the cord exposed to direct sunlight since the radiation from the sun can damage the cord.

Always leave the tail end minimum 100 meters.

Make use of a rope protector or cushion your ropes in order to protect the edges from cutting

Make sure to clean your ropes whenever needed: wash them in pure, clean water and then let them dry in a shade in order to stop the ropes from being exposed to the UV rays.

Secure the rope's end of your rope by an end knot, leaving the safety length at 1 millimeter so that you don't slip off while rappelling down to the ground.

What is a good Knot?

The ability to tie knots is one thing, but tying the knot in a proper manner is an additional. Here are some of the characteristics of a quality knot:

1. Strength

Knot efficiency, often known as knot strength is the breaking power of the rope that has knots as opposed to the same rope's strength without knots. In order to determine the efficiency of a knot one must first look at a myriad of variables, which make it more difficult to know the true significance of any particular knot.

The most common factors to consider include the length of rope used, fashion of the rope, its type of fiber you choose, the way you make the knot look before loading, whether or not the knot is loaded multiple times and how quickly you are loading the knot how long the rope has been wet or dry as well as other factors).

The effectiveness of a traditional knot is typically between 40-80 percent of the rope's initial strength. Due to knots' weakening effects (like the effects of shock load, damage and age) it is necessary for practical use to create a large safe margin of the rope chosen for the purpose it is intended to serve.

2. Security

The strength of knots is the capacity of a knot to hold its shape. It is possible for a knot to break even if the rope stays in place. Knots that stay in place even when it is exposed to many unfavorable situations is considered to be more safe than knots that aren't.

Below are the principal reasons why a knot could break and not stay in place:

*Capsizing: Capsizing, or spilling knots is when you change its form and organize its segments usually by pulling at specific edges. Capsizing a knot's structure may provide some protection against unravelling or sliding. Certain knots can be able to capsize quickly or unexpectedly when used incorrectly. In the case of make a mistake with a the reef knot (square knot) such as a capsize, it can be dangerous.

There are other occasions when individuals capsize knots in order for fastening another knot such as the "lightning process" in the creation of"the bowline knot. In general, we tie different knots such as the Carrick bent in one way after which they undergo capsizing to make a stronger and solid form.

Slide: Some knots are intended for grabbing different items. When these knots move in a similar manner to the item that is clasped, it is referred to as knot failure. Although it's not necessarily the knot that is failing however, it is still unable to fulfill its intended goal.

In the case of a railing, if you put a typical rolling hitch over the railing and then pull it parallel to the railing, it could be subject to for a period of time prior to sliding. The issue could be solved by changing the knot's tension before putting it under any force; however, it is usually required to use the use of a rope with a different material or diameter, or a knot with extra wraps.

The process of slipping occurs because the weight causes sufficient pressure to force the cord back in the knot, in towards the load. If this is allowed to take place, it eventually reaches an point at which the tail slides through the knot and makes it untidy and break. The process may get worse if knots are repeatedly attacked against solid objects such as masts or flagpoles or dragged on rough surfaces or left to slack and strain.

It is possible to slip even in knots which are fixated when first exposing the knot to excessive stress. It is possible to reduce this risk by allowing a little rope in the working tail that is beyond the knot. You can then make sure the knot is dressed and taut the knot as tight as you can prior to loading the knot. In some cases, the use of the stopper knot as a backup knot will prevent your working tail from sliding into the knot. However it's better to select a stronger knot when you see that the knot you are using tends to slide. For maximum safety, life-threatening situations usually require the use of backup knots.

3. Releasability

Each knot is different in terms of the amount of energy needed to loosen after they have been filled. Knots, such as the water's snaffle which are difficult to remove are called jamming knots or tend to "jam." However knots such as those of the Zeppelin twist, which can be unfastened by a minimum effort, are known as "non-jamming" knots.

Chapter 4: The Basic Knots

Knot Tie Below are instances of the most fundamental knots that we employ when knot-tying as well as some others that are popular knots:

1. Overhand Knot

It is the most basic knot, and the most popular one that is utilized across a variety of fields. Overhand knots are one of the most secure knots is used to tie the object, or tie another knot. However, it could make it difficult to pull off since it can be a bit difficult to untie.

This knot is helpful in stopping the ends of yarn or rope from tearing and fraying. Also, it's a safe stopping device when hand sewing. It's it is used to create macrame bracelets and climbing ropes. Climbers also use it to secure their climbs.

How to Tie an Overhand Knot

Step 1: Cross your tag's edge over your standing end of the loop to make a.

Step 2: Slide the tag's end through the loop that you have created and pull it all the length of the.

Step 3: Tie the knot by pulling on either ends.

2. Slip Knot

The knot is also known as the slip knot overhand and is one of the most popular top knots. The slip knot can be tied easily slip knot either on a rope's end or on the narrow. But, the load must only be placed on the end that is standing.

Since you are able to quickly undo the knot in a hurry, you should be certain not to use it more than to stop the knot.

How To Tie a Slip Knot

Step 1: Form an end loop of the rope.

Step 2: Make one bight at the short part.

Step 3: Slide the bight over the loop and then pull it taut.

3. Square Knot

It is also known as a the reef knot. It is considered to be one of the best knots anyone can learn to tie. It is described as a mix of two twists, which secure one another tightly in the position. It can be used to tie two strands of cord into a single cord. In the event of weight being applied to the two twists, they create little friction between the two cords.

The knot square is efficient in the process of tying two or more things together. Its initial twist pulls the items together and the second knot forms tight reinforcements surrounding the initial twist which secures everything. The knot is useful to tie bunches of wood, branches or firewood so that they are easier to transport.

In boating in boating, the reef knot can be employed for reefing and furling sails. It forms an uniform knot which is placed on the sail carefully. It is possible to use the knot while tying an a-line neckerchief, without the need to worry that it might press on your throat. If you're looking to connect multiple lengths of cord the square knot should not be recommended because other knots are much better secured and appropriate.

How to Tie a Square Knot

1. Grab each end each hand.

Step 2. Cross the cord to your right and beneath the cord to your left.

Step 3: Pull the rope you have located to your left. Cross it and then below the cord to your right.

4. Use both of your hands to grasp the other side of your cord.

Step 5: Make sure you cross the cord to the right, between the cord and above it to your left.

Step 6: Hold the cord's end to your left and place it over and beneath the cord that is on your right side.

Step 7: Secure the knot by pulling on the running ends in tandem.

4. Figure-8 Knot

The knots are typically used for rock and sailing climbing. It prevents ropes from sliding through a restraining device. It can be jammed under pressure but it's a breeze to loosen as opposed to the knot overhand which typically requires to be cut off to release.

If used in conjunction in conjunction with locking devices an appropriate rope and climbing harness the figure-8 knot can be most often used in "prusik" climbs. This allows climbers to descend as well as to ascend since the knot unjamming.

How to Tie a Figure 8 Knot

Find a suitable length of rope and cut it to be ready for tieing the figure-8 knot.

Step 1: Form a single loop by using the rope's working end.

Step 2: Slide the working portion across your sitting part. Make a second loop by crossing the working portion across your standing side.

Step 3: Insert the rope's working edge into the loop you started with.

Step 4: Pick up both ends of the rope to tie the knot in the manner you prefer.

5. Sheet Bend Knot

Sheet bends can be helpful for tieing two ropes with different diameters however, it's not secure or robust.

How to Tie a Sheet Bend Knot

Step 1: Pick up one piece of rope and create a bight with the other end.

Step 2: Take the rope's second piece and yank it over the narrow.

Step 3: Place your working part under the narrow.

Step 4. The running end is folded below the running end to make sure that either end placed on the opposite side of the knot.

Chapter 5: Bend Knots

The knots we can categorize into these types:

Bend knots

Lashings

Binding knots

Stopper knots

Hitches

Loops

This chapter we'll explore knots that bend.

What Is a Bend Knot?

It is a knot that can be used to join two ropes. The most common bend is the sheet bend.

The most powerful twist is that of the butterfly.

The Types of Bend Knots

Here are some of the kinds of bends:

1. Carrick Bend

A different name for this type of bend is the breastplate of a sailor. The knot we use is strong to join two heavy ropes, cables, and hawsers which are strained to bend. Carrick bend is a great choice for bending heavy cables. Carrick bend is particularly suitable for rope or cable that is extremely robust and long and can easily be transformed into a conventional bend. It also has a lack of jamming, which is why it is the best choice in securing heavy loads even in water or oily conditions.

This knot has an uniform curvy shape that is ideal to be used for decorating purposes such as making Coasters, trivets made of rope mats, and wall hangings. It's a near perfect shape to bend.

There are two types of Carrick twist knot: Seized and the capsized

Differences Between a Seized Carrick Bend And A Capsized One

Appearance Capsized

Seized

Structure Strong and sturdy because of the tensioning the knot. The knot ends are fastened to ensure an easier version

The weave is loosened or else, it is difficult to loosen. Simple to undo

The grip if capsized naturally it could slide off Secure

The shape varies depending on the original Carrick bent shape.

It is suitable for making climbing nets

When secured with tags that are long it can secure heavy objects well. It is ideal to pass through winches and capstans

It also counters the weakening of knots in extremely long ropes.

Variations

Because of the eight crossings in which the ropes and cording are alternately passed between the two The true Carrick bend is often referred to as a full or double Carrick bend. Variations of the bend comprise:

" Double Coin Knot": knot's tag's ends are emitted from the same side, instead of being a diagonal approach.

Single Carrick Bend: these knots may be less secure, however they're basically the exact identical. These knots include the granny, reef, thief and Sheet bend knots.

How to Tie a Carrick Bend Knot

Step 1: Take the longer rope and utilize it to make a simple loop. Place the loop on and around the rope's working ends.

Step 2: Utilizing the over and under and under sequences take the working rope of the second rope over the first loop, and then the loop itself.

The third of the ends will emerge from opposing sides of your knot. Make sure you tighten the knot by pulling at the ends. This results that the knot loses its beautiful harmony.

*If your ropes are long, be sure that you secure the ends of them in the standing portion.

2. Butterfly Bend

Also known as it's also known as Strait bend or Alpine butterfly bend. It's utilized to connect two ends of rope and is comparable in design to an Alpine butterfly loop, except it is cut. As with the butterfly loop it forms a solid knot that allows you to remove an aging or worn-out portion of rope. The bend is not jamming, which implies that it is able to be easily unfastened after an enormous load.

How to Tie the Butterfly Bend

First, create an 8-figure loop using one of your pieces of rope.

Step 2: Fold the top portion of the loop on top of the lower part.

Step 3: pull the reversed top portion of your loop down the lower half.

Step 4: Keep pulling the knot until you get to the top, then tighten the knot and ensure it safe.

Make sure you pull your loop to the right side of your loop into the lower portion of the 3rd step.

3. Reever bend

There isn't enough information about the purpose that this knot has, but it's a simple and elegant knot. Reever knots are safe and doesn't have the risk of being loosened even in the event of intermittent load. It is due to the fact that each line that crosses outside and inside the knot is clamped in 2 points inside the knot. This bend secure is ideal to attach two ropes.

How to Tie the Reever Bend Knot

Step 1. Cross the two lengths of the rope.

Step 2: Go over the rope's end to the left side, below the rope, and up over the rope itself.

Step 3: Pull the left cord across the second cord.

Step 4: Connect that cord to the bottom of it.

Step 5: Run that cord back and forth underneath it.

Step 6: Tie that knot over to the right side and pass it through the narrow.

Step 7: Pull the cord from the right edge of your knot. Then, bring it through the Bight.

Step 8. Tauten your knot.

4. Zeppelin Bend

It is a standard naval knot that is used to secure 2 ropes in a secure manner. The bend knot is comprised of two simple knots, which are woven. According to legend, this knot's name came because people would use the bend to secure Zeppelin airships. But there's no evidence that supports this theory. The benefit of the knot is the fact that it's easy to release even after an enormous weight.

Please be aware of the details of the ZEPPLIN bend as it can be mistakenly interpreted as the Hunter's bend that is less rigid.

How to Tie a Zeppelin Bend Knot

It takes two ropes to secure a bend of a zeppelin successfully.

Step 1: Begin by creating only one bight for each rope. Then, overlap them to appear as if a "9" or "6" overlap each other.

Step 2: Take the ends of each and move them over and around The upper cord must be able to cross itself while the lower cord must be below it.

Step 3: Pass each end through the middle across one another. Each end should be threaded over each one across the middle.

Step 4: Complete the Zeppelin bend by pulling the ends together.

Note: While it is more appealing to tie your knot by trimming the ends, make sure you don't leave them too long, especially in handling loads that are sensitive.

Other Bend Knots

Beer knot - this twist is great in tubular webbing. One of the most common uses for this knot is to be used in climber slings.

Adjustable bend - a bend knot that's easy to shorten or lengthen

Albright special

Sheet bend

Chapter 6: Lashings

Lashing derives from the use of whipcords to secure objects against each the other. According to the history of times the very first lashing made by humans was the holding of stones to the tree's branch, using a series of bark strips around it in order to make an ax to build by hunting. It is the same technique we use today, but the vines' strips and barks are being substituted to synthetic and natural fiber ropes.

Lashings can be defined as a set of cords designed to hold 2 or more things together. Lashings are typically used in connection with the sailing industry, scouting, containerization and cargo. Lashings are also commonly utilized on wooden poles.

Scouting and camping We use lashings in making camping tools, and for building boats for competitions and transportation too.

They also aid for advancing the process that allows bridges and towers are constructed by using ropes and wood spars. Some regions of the globe where the main method of construction remains poles, or lashing spars.

Types of Lashings

Lashings of various types comprise:

1. Square Lashing

Through this kind of lashing two spars are connected in a 90-degree angle. Lashings with squares come in different types, however they are all made up of a chain of wraps that run across the spars before extending over the lines that pass between the two spars.

How to Tie a Square Lashing

You will require a length of rope as well as 2 poles

Step 1: Take any of the poles. attach a hitch of cloves around the pole.

Step 2: Grab the loose portion of the clove hitch, and then wrap it around the rope, before wrapping the rope between the poles.

Step 3: Lay the twists, lay the rope over the outside end of the twists that preceded it on the crosspiece as well as in the wraps already attached to the second piece.

Step 4: Use your "inside-outside" sequence for wrapping your rope around poles.

Step 5: Once you've created the number of wraps you need in order to provide the strength that you need then pass the rope vertically between poles.

6. Twist the rope around the knot that is formed at the center of both poles. This is known as frapping. Make the frapping as tight as you can prior to creating a twist.

Step 7: Secure an open hitch around the edge of the cross piece in order to finish the lashing.

2. Diagonal Lashing

The lashing can be employed to tie the spars or poles in order to avoid racks. Its name is derived because the wrapping is twisted to across the spars diagonally.

We also use the diagonal lashing to spring two spars together so that they do not come into contact, as they would in an"X-brace.

How to Tie a Diagonal Lashing

Step 1: Secure one of the timber hitches around the poles at the point where they meet for a secure connection.

Step 2: On the diagonal that is opposite to knot, you can create three to four wrapping turns. Be sure the wraps are parallel one another prior to making them tight.

Step 3: Make 3 additional secure wraps on top of the initial 3, making sure to make the wraps parallel to each other.

Step 4: Perform three or four frapping turns through the middle of the poles over either wrap and then tie the clove to one pole.

3. Shear Lashing

The word is often referred to in the form of "sheer lashing" and is also known as shear lashing for two spars. It is used to join two spars which are parallel that are then extended from the same position to form thin legs in the same manner as we make an A-frame. Lashing is the process of making twists on between the poles, and making a hitch of cloves around only one leg.

How to Tie a Shear Lashing

Step 1: Start with a hitch made of cloves on the pole.

Step 2: Cut 6 wraps prior to beginning the first frame.

Step 3: Draw 2 fraps at the center on your poles.

Make use of a clove to tie loose ends. Then end the lashing by breaking the legs.

4. Round Lashing

It's also referred to in the field of vertical lashing. It's typically utilized to join two poles in order to extend the length of their respective poles. In general, it involves 2 lashings that are a reasonable distance to each other to provide extra durability. Simply put, it is not a turn of frapping. We fix either pole by the help of a clove.

How to Tie a Round Lashing

1. To start with, secure a clove over the poles.

Second step: tie your rope around the poles repeatedly according to the amount of time.

Step 3: End the lashing with an oblique hitch.

5. Tripod Lashing

It's also known as 3-spar shear lashing or GYN lashing (of eight lashings). Lashings for tripods are helpful in connecting 3 spars in order to make the tripod.

How to Tie a Tripod Lashing

*This lashing will require three poles, as well as a piece of rope

Step 1: Start by attaching a hitch of cloves to one of the poles.

Step 2: Create around 6 turns of racking on three poles as weaving in and out between the poles.

Step 3: Make 3 to 4 frapping turns across each gap.

Step 4: Close the process by attaching a clove.

5. Form The tripod is formed by crossing two poles to the outside.

Chapter 7: Binding Knots

Binding knots are one which holds two objects tightly to each other or secures just one item. Whippings, whippings, and seizings provide the same function in the knot.

But, they contain many wraps that cannot become a real knot, but they do not have characteristics of a traditional knot. Think of them as a variant of knots. In binding knots you can tuck the ends of cording beneath the turning of the knot or they join.

There are two main categories of knots: knotted-ends knots as well as friction knots. It is common to tie both the tails of the rope in order to keep knotted-end knots secure, when it comes to friction knots the friction between the windings of the rope keeps them in place.

Types of Binding Knots

The knots listed below are included in one of two categories:

1. Butcher's Knot

The main purpose of this knot of binding is for preparing meats to roast. But, it can be used for other purposes, such as you could use it to tie the loop of a parcel or packaging.

The best material is twine to tie this knot in generally 1" intervals over the roast. (Strings as well as cords will accomplish the task). The knot is easy to tighten, and you don't need to keep it in place using your hands as you tighten.

The advantages of a butcher knot is the fact that it is lesser string, and it's fast and easy to tie. Its drawback is that as long as it's safe enough to serve its purpose but it's not an ideal option when greater reliability is required. If, for instance, you want to use the knot for packaging the item, it's necessary to reinforce it by using other half-hitches and half knots.

How to Tie the Butcher's Knot

Step 1: Place the twine or cord over the roast. By putting the end of the cord at the other end of the line make an overhand knot. Pull to the taut.

Step 2: Utilize the end that is standing to form half-hitches over the tag end. An easy method of doing this is to create the loop with your fingers, then sliding it over the tag's edge.

Step 3: tighten with either of the ends, then clip the shorter end. Repeat the process at intervals of 1" along the length of your roast.

2. Half Knot

The half knot is described as the initial twist in an asymmetrical knot. In tying a half knot, the knot is tied with one side over another to make an ideal one-way symmetry knot. As this is the sole way to "bind" in a symmetrical way so it's vital to do it correctly. If you try to convert an untied half knot into the half hitch knot the knot will definitely slip. The first half knot will typically then followed by a second half knot, or even further.

Don't forget to write down where you tie the knot, i.e., left over right. This is particularly important when knotting the reef (square) knot in a proper manner because if one half-knot is attached "right over left" the second knot has to have the same knot "left across right". If you make the second half knot the same manner as the first one then you'll create"the granny knot".

Warning! Two half knots can create a good enough knot, you must be careful that you control its use. Be sure not to use the square knot created of two half knots in important loads since it's widely known for its slippage and capizing.

How to Tie a Half Knot

Step 1: Put two ends of rope on top of a desk.

Step 2: Take the other end, then connect it to the opposite.

Step 3: Place the working part between the upper and lower end for once.

Step 4: Form the half knot by fastening the rope's end.

3. Thief Knot

The knot is referred to in the form of a bread bag, or"the bag knot. It's identical to the square knot, with the open (working) ends with contrasting sides. It is believed that sailors would use the"thief knot" (mostly using the knot with its ends hidden) to keep their valuables in a bag called a ditty.

If anyone else had access to it, then there are likely to be a high chance that the "thief was using the common reef knot for tying back the bag. This shows evidence of tampering, therefore the reason for its designation.

When properly knotted and properly, the tails are to be placed on opposing edges, in a diagonal manner. The knot for the bread bag can be easily loosened and has a lower degree of reliability than the flimsy reef knot.

How to tie the Thief Knot Step 1: Create an elongated bight with one end of the rope.

Step 2. Slide the second part of the bight through, then wrap it around the other side to wrap around that original piece of bight.

3. Fold the running side towards its standing end.

Fourth step: pull the lever to the tightening.

4. Granny Knot

Granny knots are one of the forms that is a Carrick bend that is made up of several half knots, each one of which is placed over one another. It's also referred to false, lubbers or calf or the booby knot. It is thought to be derived from the way that the knot was utilized in granaries to secure the necks of bags. The ends of the knot have a vertical incline towards the end that is standing.

The benefit of knots is that it creates the basis for surgeon's knot.

The drawback is that it is susceptible to slippage in heavy loads, and then become loose easily, and is unstable and susceptible to jamming when it is tightened too much.

Uses

The knot can be used to tie the cord to an object or surgical procedure, for tying up packages informally, creating macrame bracelets and holding crafting objects without gluing them down, before using staples, pins or glue as well as tying shoelaces and ribbons among others.

How to Tie a Granny Knot

Step 1: Make the loop open by tying the rope. Position the rope's working side upside down.

Step 2: Insert another rope through the loop just below the standing end.

Step 3: Cross the 2nd working edge above the standing end, and below the working end at first.

Step 4. Cross back to the beginning working edge, and then slide the loop into.

5. Make sure the knot is tight.

5. Surgeon's Knot

The knot is sometimes referred to as Double Surgeon's Knot. It's one of the most popular knots that are easy to create to connect cords that have the same or different dimensions. For ensuring that it is properly sealed you can tighten it by pulling onto each of the four braids.

The knot is similar to the knot used for reefs, but the initial knot part has an additional "pass-through'. It is less likely that the line will slip when you tie the knot after you've completed the knot.

The pass-through created around the base aids in keeping the knot in place as you tie the other portion in the knot. The knot also becomes more resistant to being unfastened.

Based on the stitch you choose to use The surgeon's knot may serve as a useful way of joining the beading tails thread, for example when you add new threads or when tying the threads. If used this way it requires adequate space between the beads before putting on the knot.

The surgeon's knot is great when paired with the elastic cord. Bead embroidery is a technique where it is used at the very ends of a thread in order to make a knot that is not able to slip into the beading base.

How to Tie a Surgeon's Knot

Step 1: cross the left-hand strand of cord over the right strand. Take the right-side cord and tie it around the left strand, continue to lead it over the top of the middle.

Step 2. While holding the strand of the earlier step remaining in your palm Cross it over and to the opposite strand and repeat. There should be two wraps of the Strand.

Step 3: Take the string on the right side, then cross it over to the left strand, then wrap it around the knot's central point before sliding across the knot. Make sure the knot is secured by pulling all the way to both edges of the cording.

The knot can be strengthened by increasing the strength of your knot by adding a few drops of transparent nail polish or GS-Hypo Cement to the over.

Chapter 8: Stopper Knots

Stopper knots are a type of knots we use to secure a cord temporarily or to prevent an untied cord from falling into the grommet. Stopper knots are placed around the stand or near the end of the cord.

The stopper knot is used at the ends of ropes to stop them unraveling In this case it will function as whipping knot. In contrast when you tie a knot on the rope's end to stop it from moving through a device for belaying or rappelling block, hole or keep it from falling into a different knot it acts as a handle for a leash.

The stopper knot can be called an alternative knot if it is knotted on the outside of a knot that is not tied on the stand end. When you tie the end of your rope to the part that is standing to prevent unravelling the knot, by preventing the tail from slipping back into the knot. This is a kind of protection against a knot failing. Similar functions can be observed for knots used in climb rescue and rope safety, as well as various other emergency situations that require lifesaving measures.

Types of Stopper Knots

Let's now take a examine the different types of knots that stoppers can be found below:

1. Monkey's Fist

Also known as the monkey's foot The knot has been around for a long time in which it is used to add an extra weight at the top of a heaving rope to allow easy throwing of the heaving rope exactly where it's required. Heaving line is a lightweight rope that is that is tossed from the dock to ship, to carry another very heavy rope into the proper place. It is beneficial in door stopper weights and decorative curtain tie backs keys, keychain fobs and Cufflinks. The rope's weight and the amount of turns that you turn determine the length of your knot.

In the case of decorative purposes, an spherical piece like a tennis ball the golf ball, or marble are typically placed at the center of the knot in order to create an ideal round form and provide more mass on the knot.

It is also possible to use the monkey's fist knot to skydive as well as climbing rocks. When metal rings may damage soft rocks, climbers can hammer the monkey's fist knot in cracks in the rock to support the body weight. Additionally, because of the more stable, firmer quality and also because it's much more robust than the old rope handle used on parachutes, skydivers often utilize them for their skydiving adventures.

How to Tie Monkey's Fist Knot

Step 1: Pick up the longest-running part of the rope, and make three wraps with your fingers. Once you have the first set of wraps firmly by their own weight, make 3 additional rotations that go out of the first 3 wraps.

The running end should be positioned across on one end of the original set of wraps in order to finish the process. This will ensure that the running edge is in the correct position to proceed with the next step. You will need to slip the rope's trail through the previous wraps.

Step 2: After passing through the knot create 3 wraps in the sequence of turns that you made earlier in the process. Make sure that every step contains an equal turns.

Finalizing: You may insert a round object within the center of the wraps. Alternatively, you could tie into the standing end of the rope using knots for a stopper near the end or with no. Begin tightening the process in a gradual manner, working each wrap starting from the end of the stopper knot then finishing with the remaining rope's ending.

Be aware that for the first two wraps, make sure you are pulling gently.

*The monkey's hand is repeatedly worked until you reach your desired size. To tighten the whole knot, you can use an awl or small screwdriver to assist you in the.

2. Barrel Knot or Blood Knot

The barrel knot to connect pieces of monofilament nylon line together in order to maintain the strength of the line. It is best suited for the situation when you've taken fishing lines of different sizes and lengths that were discarded along the lake, beach or the riverbank and you want to make a more durable and more long-lasting line to use to fish or for any other type of activity. The blood knot can also be used blood knot to sail as the decorative knot for a stopper.

How to Tie a Blood Knot

Step 1: Cover both ends of the cords so that they meet. Then, twist one cable over the other for five turns. Then, lead your running cord back into the middle, where both lines are crossed.

2. Rework similar steps by wrapping the final end in the exact amount of turns that are in the reverse direction.

Step 3: Pull gently cords with opposing directions to allow the turns to be joined and then secure the knot. Cut the ends close to the knot.

3. Stevedore Knot

This knot is sometimes referred to as an inverse number 8 knot. It is usually tied near the end of the rope. The theory is that Stevedores (dockworkers) employed the knot for offloading and taking their boats to dock.

Massive blocks were needed for lifting and lowering cargo onto and off of the ship. This required big stopper knots to prevent ropes from getting caught in the blocks. The stevedore knot will remain in place even when it is loose, and does not cause jamming. The knot is tied much the same manner as it is tied in the form of a figure-8 knot (hence its name) however, the running ends create an additional loop around the stand end prior to sliding it back into its knot in exactly the same manner as the figure-8 knot.

Other Stopper Knots

Ashley's knot for the stopper

Double overhand knot

Slip knot

Figuring of the 8 knot

Chapter 9: Hitches

The knot we use is for securing a cord an object, typically the post, the spar, rail, or rings.

Types of Hitches

Here are some examples of commonly used knots for a hitch:

1. Trucker's Hitch

A majority of truckers utilize the knot to secure heavy load. It lets you use a rope with great force secure and safely. In time it can harm a rope as it requires tension.

It is particularly evident when you secure the knot on precisely the same spot on the rope over and over. If you'd like your rope to last change the position of your knot often or use regular rope replacements to ensure that the knot isn't damaged.

Truckers use their hitch to attach large items like a boat or canoe boat onto the roof racks of a car, and also to attach trailer items. The hitch can also be useful to suspend a hammock and pulling up tarpaulins or for other boating, climbing tasks.

One thing to note about the knot is the fact that it may cause damage to the item you are trying to tie down if the ropes are pulled too tight; the most common instance is as you pull the tarpaulins.

Variations

The majority of the variations are pretty similar to the basic knot. every one of them has a three-to-1 grip for a secure hitch, as well as the knot on top. A few differences include replacing the figure 8 by using an alpine butterfly, or bowline to create a tight knot. Other knots may use a basic twist of the rope or slip knot.

How to Tie a Trucker's Hitch Knot

For a practice knot, you'll require the appropriate length of rope as well as an object like a hook carabiner, ring or other circular item.

Step 1: Form the bight by using rope, and tie it into a figure-eight maneuvering knot.

Step 2: Turn the end of the run over the chosen object and then slip it into the loop at the bottom of the figure-eight knot.

Step 3: Tighten the knot by pulling on the running portion.

Step 4: Attach two half-hitches for securing the knot.

2. Buntline Hitch

The principal function of this knot is to connect the rope with an object. It involves twisting the cord around the object and then fastening to the standing portion to the cord. The buntline hook is straightforward to tie, and extremely safe.

It's believed to be generally more effective than two-half hitches, but it can jam when it is used to handle heavy load. In addition, it is not possible to secure the knot in the midst of a burden.

The knot was first tied to attach an edging to the bottom of sail. It was extremely convenient because the sail's flapping increased the tension of the knot and made it even safer.

The knot is used today for different purposes. It is the most common knot that can be used for connecting ropes with loops, pilings eyes, and rings. The knot is appropriate for moderate load and in situations where the use of a knot that is partially permanent is needed. When the knot is exposed to a lot of pressure and pressure, it can be difficult to loosen. The knot can also be utilized in the tying of neckties.

Variations

The hitch is available in a alternative known as the slipped form that is a lot more flexible. It is more resistant to jamming and it is ideal for times the times when you require a short-term hitch that's safe and also.

How to Tie a Buntline Hitch

In order to demonstrate how to do this, we'll attach ropes to the ring of a huge size.

Step 1: Insert the rope inside the rings (if it is an upright, wrap the rope in) Then, twist it around the upper part of the ring.

Step 2: Grab the end of the run and then pass the running end around, both below and over the standing portion for the figure-8 shape.

Step 3: slide the end of the run into the loop that you have just made.

Step 4: pull on the end until it is taut.

3. Diamond Hitch

This type of lashing can be utilized to tie down a variety of things, mainly in the horse packing industry like securing a pair of boxes for packing, bags or other equipment to the foundation. The typical method of fastening this knot requires an appropriate foundation prepared using a minimum of two anchorage points as well as a rope to tie the objects on top of the base. Diamond hitches come in two varieties that are single and double.

The principal function of the diamond hitch is the ability to fix the object to a pack saddle set on the back of animals like a donkey, horse or mule (alpacas and llamas too are often utilized).

It is also possible to use this knot to create a stylish effect on a truck's bed, or on a plane, with loads fixed to the.

Other Types of Hitches

The hitch on the barrel

Anchor hitch

Hitch for the cow

Clove hitch

Sailor's hitch

Chapter 10: Loop Knots

It is a type of knot that forms an elongated loop which is then permanently fixed. The knot is created under two situations - by knotting a loop inside the bight on your rope is knotted or when the tail end of cording is secured with the point that is standing on the same cord.

As opposed to a hook, this knot is an unbreakable loop using the ability to keep its design. It doesn't matter if it is attached to the object or it isn't. It means you are able to cut a loop knot out of the item and it'll keep its form.

Types of Loop Knots

It is possible to classify loop knots in different types of heads according to their shape. Here are the different types of loops:

Single loop knots

Double loop knots

Adjustable loop knots

Midline loop knots

End (end) knots in loops

Knots with a fixed loop

Single Loop Knots

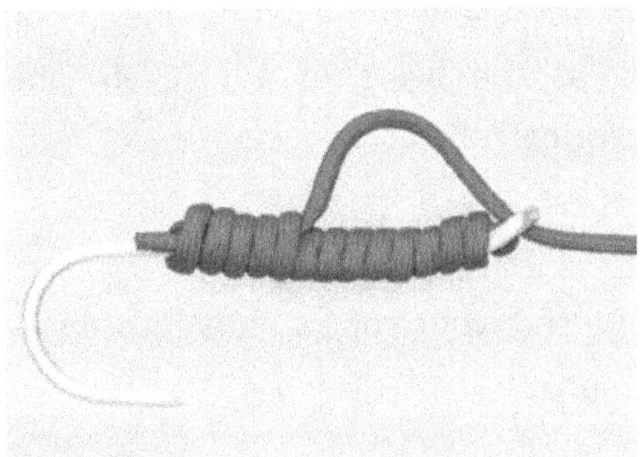

If you have to connect objects to a rope of rope (such for rock climbing) or to toss ropes over the object, such as the post (to secure your boat to, say, anchor your boat) A single loop knot can be quite useful.

Below are some of the best instances of the loop knot:

1. Egg Loop Knot

The knot is mostly used in fishing where it firmly holds soft baits against the hook's shank. Many refer to it by the name of the "roe" fishing knot, or bumper knot.

This knot makes eggs useful when you are fishing for salmon and steelhead, however you can also use it for securing dough baits as well as the livers of a chicken when fishing for catfish.

How to Tie An Egg Loop Knot

Step 1: Insert your rope's ends into an eye on the hook.

Second step: wrap the end three times across the hook, and then over the standing part.

Step 3: Perform nine more turns using the same rope before moving it over the loop.

Step 4: Pull the loop made at the top and then twist it over the stand end.

5. Turn 5 additional rotations with the same loop. Finally, keep the longer end in order to tighten it.

Step 6: Form an opening by pulling the rope, after which you can secure the egg by placing it in the opening.

2. Diamond (Lanyard) Knot

It's also known as the knife lanyard knot Bosun's Whistle knot, or the friendship knot. The diamond knot is used for a sturdier permanent loop in the middle of a rope or a small cord (such for paracord). Also, you can make use of lanyards and leather for the knot.

How to Tie a Diamond Knot

Step 1: Begin with forming a loop and then begin to wrap this rope.

Step 2: Slide one of your ropes over the loop you've just made.

Step 3: Leap to the end of the loop in an upward direction. Then cross it over the first loop.

Step 4: Grab the longer loop. Then make the knot tighter by pulling the two ends.

3. Spider Hitch Loop Knot

This knot loop is great to make a sturdy double line. Also, it is useful for surfing, and you could modify it to make the web-based rig. One thing to know about the spider-hitch loop knot is that it allows you to decrease friction by moistening the line using saliva before pulling out the end to make an extremely secure, strong knot.

How to Tie a Spider Hitch Loop Knot

Step 1: Wrap the untied end of the line in your thumb turn it around 5 times the line (make 15 turns if using a fishing line that is braided).

Step 2. The line's ends are crossed towards the back of the loop. move it across the loop.

3. Yank the loop's end. loop.

Fourth step: Pull on either end of the knot to secure it.

Step 5: Cut the tail and turn it around to seal it.

Double Loops

Double loops are typically more secure and durable than a single loop because they provide double grip for the object. If there is an emergency situation, such as example, when it requires lifting or lowering someone the double loop knot could be utilized to serve as the strapping. There are a variety double loop knots among them, we've listed in the following sections:

1. French Bowline Knot

The knot is sometimes referred to as the Portuguese bowline. It is a safe and useful knot that makes two loops. It's similar to the standard Bowline knot in that it has two loops that can be adjusted.

This knot is utilized to secure mooring lines linking two ropes with each and creating shackles that are made up (if you need to) for rigging, as well to create a harness. The Portuguese bowline can also be used to support heavy loads without getting jammed.

Be aware that this knot must be loaded only downwards. If you try to load it in another direction, it's likely unravel. Additionally, be sure you equally load both loops so that the knot doesn't become unstable.

How to tie a French Bowline Knot 1: Make a tiny overhand loop in the middle of the rope, by connecting the working part with the part that is standing.

Step 2. Slide your working end over the loop you've just constructed. Make the loop according to the size you prefer.

Step 3. Feed your work part into the smaller loop and then guide it up over the second loop.

Step 4: Double-over the part that is standing, and then put it back in the loop.

Step 5: Close the knot by securing it and then pulling it downwards.

2. Bowline on a Bight

This variation is similar to the bowline knot, which double loops. This creates an extremely solid loop (bowline) within the middle of the line. If you want to have two loops on the ends of the rope which is not slippy and you do not have an open end in reach, a bowline of a bight is an option.

The knot can be helpful in times of need when you have to lift or lower someone, without the knot getting caught or jamming.

As you climb, the knot may also be utilized for a strong toe-hold at the middle of rope.

Be aware that if you need to you want to work on both loops with different sizes.

How to tie the Bowline On A Bight Knot

Step 1: Draw An "eye" or loop with the rope.

Step 2: Take the free end, and then slide it over the eye in two loops under the eye.

Step 3: Pull the open free side down beneath the double loop.

Step 4. Make sure you cross the free end of the double loop, then continue up until you are above the eye.

Step 5: Secure the stand line and squeeze the double loop in order to tie the knot.

Double loop knots are another option.

Spanish bowline

" Double Figure 8 Knots

Adjustable (Sliding) Loop Knots

It's extremely helpful to learn how to tie a knot that is adjustable to tie your camping gear to a pole to making friendship bracelets.

As much as there is a wide variety of adjustable knots, mastering the slip and sliding knot will provide you with an excellent foundation for every adjustable-knot-tying need.

The knots with adjustable tension further down:

1. Poacher's Knot

The knot is also known as double-overhand noose, strangle or a two-turn (or the double) scaffold. The knot is identified as a double hand knot that is woven around a bight. Poachers would use the knot for catching animals, including birds. wild animals. That's why the designation.

The knot of the poacher is a sturdy knot we employ for securing an object rope to for forming a simple snare to join a hand ascender to an ankle loop. The distinctive thing about this knot is the fact that you are able to construct it with the help of slippery ropes such as those constructed from Spectra as well as Dyneema. The strangle snare can become stuck once loaded and is difficult to remove.

How do you tie the knot of Poacher's Knot?

Step 1: Take the tag's end and wrap it around a piece of rope.

Step 2. Twist the end a second time using the same method.

Step 3: Move the tag's upper end towards you.

Step 4: Slide this end through the two loops you made.

5. Yank the other ends to tighten your knot.

Be sure that you don't miss step 2 like most people skip it. If you wrap the tag's end one time, you'll end up with an overhand knot that isn't very safe. You can also make an end knot using the tag's end, if you have enough left to provide added protection.

2. Scaffold Knot

The knot on the scaffold is similar to the poacher's knot, but it comes with an additional turn. Also known as a triple knot overhand. The knot forms a sturdy loop, which can slide like an overhand noose. It can be positioned tightly around a railing or bar, or other similar item.

If you use the lining that is that is referred to as a thimble it will protect the knot from wear and tear due to chafing, because it forms what sailors call"a "hard eye". There are thimbles available in diverse sizes from boat and handlers of boats.

How to tie a Scaffold Knot

Step 1: Make a loop around the back of your rope. make use of the working part to turn it about the stand and it.

Step 2: Retrace your steps toward the loop that you made by following the steps above, and tie 3 loops that wrap around the line. (Note that if you are making this knot in order to tie the loop onto something, such as a pole, you should begin by doing this method).

Step 3: After you've completed your 3rd turn, slide your working edge through the spaces created by the wraps and run parallel to your standing piece.

Step 4: Pull with the work end to tie the knot.

Other Adjustable Loop Knots

The Hangman's (noose) knot French bowline and running bowline. Slip knot, handcuff knot.

Mid Line Rope Loops

They can also be referred to for their open knots. Midline loops of rope are formed by looping the other end of the rope and then knotting each end of the rope to make an equilateral square knot, leaving an open loop. Midline rope knots are:

1. Handcuff Knot

It is also known as hobble knot. It is used to tie two loops into the middle of rope, which can be used as the equivalent of handcuffs. However, because this knot does not have an inherent locking mechanism and is therefore not suitable to restricting.

However, it is possible to make a number of knots overhand using the end-of-line knots to tie the knot securely. Making the hobble knot is simple (and fast) as you could utilize rope, webbing lines, paracord or strings to tie knots.

Handcuff knots are effective in pulling carcasses from animals, keeping animals or horses in order to prevent their feet from wandering and securing oars to each other and securing them to rails on boats.

How to tie a Handcuff Knot

Step 1: Make use of your rope to make two loops.

Step 2. Overlap your loops so that they are running each other across each other's opposite sides.

Step 3: Take hold of the ends that are standing and pull the loops to the size you prefer.

Step 4: Secure the knot with a tight pull.

Be aware that you can alter the length of your loops by pulling onto them lightly to get an appropriate dimension in the final step.

2. Spanish Bowline Knot

The Spanish bowline is made up of two sturdy loops that resemble the butterfly.

You can employ as a sling to lift or lower those who are stranded, wounded or just overloaded.

The size can be adjusted of the loops before tying the knot to a full extent. This knot is easy to tie and does not cause jamming.

How To Tie the Spanish Bowline Knot

Step 1: Make an arc with the rope and leave the two tails hanging down below the loop.

Step 2. Make sure the loop is folded lower than the remaining parts (hanging the tails).

Step 3. Make sure to fold the loop on your right over the loop on the left side, and then cross the left loop on the right side, creating two loops: one central loop, and two side loops.

Step 4: Fold both ends of the center loops upwards, forming the side loops. Finally, pull them apart.

Step 5: Pull the lever to make it tighter.

Other Midline Rope Loops

The double figure eight knot dropping loop, alpine butterfly knot the figure 8 directional, figure 8 follow through, and bowline in a bight.

Terminal (End) Loops Knots

The knots we use are mostly used to connect fishing gear to make it exact. They also make use of terminal knots to hold cattle in place and secure the animals in their place.

Below are different kinds knots for end loops:

1. Non-Slip Knot

The knot can also be called the mono knot that is non-slip, the non-slip mono loop or Kreh. If we employ the knot that is non-slip for lures, it stays flexible and allows the lure the ability to move more easily within the water.

How to Tie a Non-Slip Knot

Step 1: At approximately 1" at the point of the line you are fishing on create an overhand knot.

Step 2: Insert your knot over the hook eye. utilize the working end of the line to complete at least 4-5 rotations around the stand end. Slide the tag end over the knot that is overhand.

Step 3: Stiffen your knot by soaking it in water and then gently pull on the tag's end so that the wraps stay loose.

Step 4: Sew the knot by pulling both the hanging part of the loop and the standing one opposite ways. Trim the end of the tag.

2. The Perfection Loop

Also called the Angler's Loop. The perfect loop is a crucial knot for fishing. Many (especially women and fishermen) consider it to be the most effective fishing loop and many think it helps in fishing success.

It can be useful to secure one loop to the top of fishing lines. The knot is very simple to tie and is also being durable and efficient. The other benefit of the perfect loop is that it allows you to reduce the size of the loop in the event of need.

The perfect loop is nearly perfect, however it's not ideal when you have to remove the knot because it can jam very easily.

How to Tie The Perfection Loop

Step 1: Take the tag's end, then pass it through the gap behind your standing portion for a loop to the apex of your rope as well as fishing line.

Step 2: Make a new loop with the line you created previously mentioned in step one. Once your line is securely to the ground, make an additional loop. This one is different, in you'll need be able to connect it with the loop that you previously created.

Step 3: Secure the tag's end in place before going through the second loop the first.

Step 4: Pull the second loop Then, clip off the tag's excess end.

Other Terminal Loop Knots

Poacher's Knot, running bowline, Rapala knot, Bimini twist Honda knot Bowline knot and The Hangman's (Noose) knot, and surgeon's loop.

Chapter 11: Ropes Has Parts

Are you surprised to know that ropes are made up of elements? Sure, there are parts and in this article, we'll be discussing the components that let you learn more about the rope you're trying to tie.

Bight

Bights are the bends of the rope.

Loop

Loops are created by crossing the rope with a cross-over and the result is the loop.

Over Hand Loop

It happens where the end of the working rope is crossed over by the stand end. This is the one of the rope in your hands which you're using at this moment. The standing end is the one which isn't being used and could be lying placed on the ground or in the other. Once the stand end is taken up, and the working one falls, it's not the same thing as it was known as. The end which is on ready and active in the present time is considered to be the working end. Any end not in use in the present time is considered to be the standing end. This ensures that there's no confusion.

Under Hand Loop

It happens when the work of the rope comes between the end that is standing of the rope.

Types of Knots

Bend

This knot is utilized to fix the two ends of the rope.

Binding

The knotting method is the one you use to knot an object in such a way to tie the object in a secure way.

Decorative

The knots of this type are typically used to beautify the space. Tieing is performed using various methods to enhance the surrounding.

Hitch

When you think trying to tie a knot on the dock, a tree or even an rings. This knot is used to tie it to the tree or what you'd like to tie it.

Basic Knots

In this article, we will be discussing some of the fundamental knots that form the basis of knot tying. They are knots used to illustrate and explain the basic step-by-step techniques for knot tying. There are a lot of items that form part of other knots, and some others provide the basic structure the basis of. The figure 8 contains a variety of more knots which are extremely important.

There are a few terms that we use for knots such as knots like the Overhand Knot, Half

Hitch as well as the Half Knot that are most often misunderstood and frequently considered to be substituted. They are usually used in conjunction together with Slip Knot as well as the Noose knot.

Figure 8 Knot

An unbinding, fast and simple stopper knot.

How to tie the knot is to use the working part, the end of the rope you hold at this moment. Then, you pass it over itself. This forms an elongated loop. The working end is placed under the rope. You can tie the knot by running it down the loop.

It is the Figure 8 Knot provides a quick and easy to apply stopper knot that can stop the line from sliding away from view. The figure 8 knot stops your rope from sliding into an opening. It can include a carabineer or a belay device. After you have pushed it out of your hole are able to put it in a hanger or give it something. If you've tied a knot tied, apply the figure-8 knot to tie it very near to it, so it is possible to keep those knots from being pulled loose.

It is among the most simple stopper knots you can tie. It is effortless to remove even if you've used it to transport a large burden. It is notable it's less bulky than other knots for stopping.

Half Hitch Knot

Useful to secure rope around objects and then return it to itself.

It is necessary to create an arc around the object which you want to wrap it around. Then, you can pass on one side of rope across another end. The two ends are supposed to connect.

It is then necessary to tighten it into the Half Hitch which is made to hold a weight, exactly like an Arrow which is at the stand end.

Then, you would take the two ends of the rope, and then cross them under each other.

The Half Hitch Knot to look as an overhand knot, and change it back into how a typical Half Hitch should look similar to.

Two Half Hitches

The very first Half Hitch Knot that you have to tie will usually be tied with a subsequent or a third tie. The loop will become more durable. It is well-known that Two Half Hitches can lead to the creation of a full "Hitch" It is nevertheless recommended to take the rope, and then wrap it over the bollard or post the bollard the second time in order to make an Round Turn and Two Half Hitches. This provides you with the most secure grip, and gives you a strong grip on the weight that you carry while you tie half Hitches.

Noose Knot

The loop will become tighter when pulled.

It is also used as an hunting snail. It is first necessary to create a loop at the middle of the rope in the manner shown in the image above. Transfer the rope that you have looped over the rest of rope. Place a bight on the end that is standing of the rope inside the loop created and place it directly on the rope.

Expand the bight, then wrap it over the item you intend to attach it to. Then pull the opposite end to tighten the bight.

Don't confuse yourself with the other kinds of knot, the basic Noose Knot is very much identical in its structure, when you compare it to that of the Slip Knot, except that the bight supposed to insert comes from the longer end instead of the shorter end. The majority of the time, it's always been utilized to snare animals when you want to capture smaller animal.

The majority of people use knots with the Noose Knot - this is often used to make the first loop to cast on. It is usually tied with the Noose. This knot is referred to as an Slip Knot. There are a variety of uses that you can make use of to do this, for instance the need to have the control first of the thread when making a knot for a bundle.

There's a link to The Hangman's Knot and the simple Noose in addition to it being a number of turns wrapped around the loop. Its benefit of being able the ability to hang was for humanitarian reasons: The proper use of the knot was intended for the risk of someone falling off their neck, which can lead to a quick death.

The process employed to make Noose Knotting is to take one of the bights from the longer end and tie it in the loop. It is possible to achieve the similar result using the short ends of the object around it and using the shorter end to ensure you are able to tie half Hitch to the long end.

The Noose knot isn't described as the Hangman's Knot but it definitely is deadly. It is not recommended to make it tightly when it's around an individual's neck, due to the impact it could have on necks. It is possible for the knot to bind. it can severely hinder blood flow.

Overhand Knot

This is the most basic of single-strand stopper Knots.

In this article, I'll show you to tie an overhand knot. Make loops at the ends of your rope. Then, you should go over the top of the rope that you tied the loop by the loop you constructed.

Take the end was tucked in the loop you made to be tightened to form the Overhand Knot. It can also be used to create an easy stopper knot. It can be tied through the hole, and once it's done this will stop the rope from going through that hole. Then, you can utilize the rope to pull the object around or whatever you wish to do with your object or the rope.

Overhand Knot Overhand Knot was described as one of the single-string stopper knots that are the easiest to knot. The knot can utilized to stop the rope's end of rope from unravelling.

It has one benefit that the knot on the overhand can provide as a stopper. Among other knots for stopping this is among those that are securely tied against an object or knot.

Chapter 12: Sheet Bend

It's the joining of two ropes which are different, or have a similar dimensions.

Two ropes are in use The one that is heavy and the other one isn't so you need to join them. The goal is to create an elongated loop with the heavier rope. You then have to hold it in one hand.

Take the rope that is thinner and put it into the loop on the larger rope you've made, then remove it the back of the thick rope.

Now, you need to put the rope that is smaller through the middle, and after that, you should put it back in place to repeat the process a second time.

The other knots that are suggested are designed for joining which have equal dimensions. For example, the Sheet Bend also known as Weaver's Knot is highly recommended for joining two ropes that are not equal in size. Be sure to use more thick ropes for basic Bight. But, it's well when both ropes are the same in size.

If you intend to utilize ropes to carry a massive haulage, no matter what it is then you must extend the ends of the ropes more long in order to allow to expand and allow for ease of movement.

Becket Hitch Becket Hitch is very similar to the knot for sheet bend. But, it's an "Hitch" This type is not a knot that joins two ropes. What does it do is tie the rope to the Becket. The tinier Rope is referred to as Becket while the bigger Rope is tied to it by a backet Hitch.

Slip Knot

Simple loop on the rope's end and it will loosen at the ends are pulled.

This time, I'll show how to make this slip knot. This knot is actually a stopper for temporary use knot, and isn't commonly used for starting knitting.

The first step is create a loop toward the ending of the rope you're working with. You can then decrease the diameter so that to create a bight toward the edge of your rope. You can then tuck the bight have created into the loop that you made in the rope. Then make sure to tighten the knot. It is possible to use the knot for a an interim stopper knot. It is easy to loosen.

There's a resemblance in the Slip Knot and Noose Knot when it comes to the construction, but however, in this case the bight you inserting is constructed out of the shorter end is still pending, and is not on the other end of your rope. The Slip Knot, which is one of all the knots, is among knots which are often tied that is mainly utilized when knitting the initial loop while casting. It is often referred to as a slip knot and is often tied in a knot that is a noose.

Square Knot

An easy way to join two ropes, which are composed of two half knots.

I'll show the proper way to tie a square knot, also known as the reef knot.

If you have two ropes, you can pass one rope over each other, creating an x-shaped letter, and then it is necessary to pull one rope under the rope that is facing in reverse.

The rope was pushed down should be pulled to the front. Next, you should put the rope which was moved forward on top of the rope that was not pushed to the back.

It is recommended to place the rope over others, and the one rope pushed will sit on top of the other rope, and the second rope that was pulled would be placed underneath the blue rope, as seen above. The red rope should be passed through the bight as depicted and make sure to tighten the rope.

To make a more secure knot, create another half knot.

The knot was intended to function as the binding knot. you should tie it in the correct material on an uncurved surface. The initial Half Knot that was done could bind, however, you shouldn't be sure, which is the reason why we recommend to use the knot in a half.

Stopper Knot

Celtic Button Knot

This knot is often referred to the single-strand diamond knot. The way to create it. You will need create two clock loops which is achieved using the rope to make a loop by twisting the rope at one end before moving it across the back of the rope.

Make a second loop, but this time it must come from the opposite end of the rope. Take it into exactly the same position as the initial loop constructed.

After that, you'll be required to pull the second portion of the rope and run this through the loop created. First, you need to ensure that the second loop is able to partially extends over the initial lop which was created. You then pass the opposite portion of the rope through the second loop constructed, with the second loop over the first loop. Pass it through the first loop before bringing it into the second loop in order that it is placed on top of the first loop. You then go through the loop you made before and drag it until it forms a new loop.

Then, you'll pull the ends of the rope that is on the other end, move it through the new loop before passing it through the loops that are visible before pulling it out into the space next to it and drag it along the opposite ends of the rope until it is evenly tightens. There may be some tension in the knots which is why you need to ensure that you set to tighten them up by extending the loops you have created prior to pulling the ropes back at a gentle pace from each end.

The knot can be used as decorative purposes, and also in single-strand bracelets as the knot for a stopper, or as a way to embellish the bracelets you own.

Double Over Hand Knots

The rope should be wrapped twice around your index finger. as you pull it from your index finger you will have created the loop.

Next, you should pass the second side of the rope inside the loop you've made. Pull each end of the rope until you've reached the double-end knot.

The knot that you choose to tie will look as follows. The knot is functional and aesthetic usages. It's as a stopper knot. It is a good knot for climbs, boating and sailing. It is also the foundation for knots that are useful, including the double fisherman's knot or the double noose over the hand.

The Barrel Knots

The knot is very similar with the double-over head knots. It is often mistaken for the latter because of their level of similarity.

Take a small piece of rope, tie it to your index fingers for three times. Then, you'll need to cut it off from the remainder. Take the end that is working of the rope and put over the loop which has been made and then make sure the knot is tight by moving between the two sides of the rope until it becomes tight.

Similar to it's counterpart, the overhead knot also has two distinct functions. It's mostly used for to climb and is also used for a stopper knot.

Stevedore Knot

Then, you would grab the working part of the rope, create a bend and then take it over across the opposite side of the rope.

Two loops are created by wrap the rope transferred to the other end of the rope, across the loop made. Then wrap it around the rope twice. In the second loop you have created, wrap the rope around the first loop. Then, you can pass the rope through the original loop.

After passing the rope around that loop, you are able to make it tighter by moving the wrap until the loop is tightened. Cut off any excess rope left over and melt it over fire to stop the rope from falling off. This will result in a lovely single strand stopper. It's great on lanyards. It makes an extremely strong and sturdy single-strand stopper knot is used to block your rope from going over different things.

The Monkey's Fist

Make sure you hold one side of the rope, be sure the other length isn't too long Then, grab the opposite end of the rope, which is the one that stands and roll it around your middle and index fingers 2 times, creating two loops.

You would then make two times over the made loop. This involves making the other end the rope, and then moving it through the loop twice, making sure you spread your hands slightly wide enough to allow the rope to go across from the bottom.

It is possible to purchase a tiny ball bearing, and place it between the spaces which will be made as you make your second loop. After that, you remove your fingers slowly to prevent the ball from falling and the rope from falling.

You then place the rope inside the holes created by your index finger and then move it through the other end through the second hole made by your middle finger. You then take it back to run it through the initial loop, and at the other end to go through the loop again.

Once you've finished it, make sure you adjust the cord that is left, it will be more similar to tightening the knot in its entirety. It is necessary to pull on one loop, and then adjust the second section of the loop until it is tightened. Repeat this process until the knot is snug. In effect, you're taking the excess from your monkey's fist towards the opposite.

Take care where you're doing the pulling to ensure that you do not end up moving back and forth, in the hope of accomplishing anything. You will require a little amount of time to become comfortable with.

The monkey's fist knot. You may decide to trim the edges or simply pass through your fist. The knot has a variety of other artistic applications and uses.

It is a great way to put weight on one side of the rope to ensure that it can be thrown onto something.

Fishing Knots

In the case of fishing, or other forms of fishing, the knot for fishing is the primary component of the whole system of fishing. There are times when you will choose the wrong rod for fishing but you'll nevertheless get fish. There are times when you might find the wrong reel or the wrong line but you still can be successful in catching fish, but if you make a mistake with your knot when you tie it improperly, you're not going to fish since the line is bound break.

It is then possible to lose the fishing catch, and then loose the hook, and that isn't likely to be a pleasant day. Therefore, if you're new to fishing and would like to be aware of the perfect knots to tie and correctly, I'll be showing the exact knot in this book. how to tie it.

Chapter 13: How To Tie The Nail Knot

Over time Over time, the Nail Knot has been tested and has become a well-known knot that is used to connect fly line and leader. Instead of nailing using a tiny hollow tube (coffee stirrer sticks are a good choice) works well.

Nail Knot Tying Instructions

Use a nail or a hollow tube over the top of the fly line.

Place the end of the down section of the leader to the line as well as the tube. Add an extra 10-12 inches at the tag's end to secure the Knot.

Create up to eight tightly around wraps working from left to right and returning around the leader the nail or tube. The tag ends should be inserted into the tube or into the hole which was created by the nail, and eliminate the tube.

Make sure to pull the tag's end in such a way that you can tighten the coils, then pull the leader and tag until it sits the knot securely on the fly line.

Take off the end of the tag that is closest to knot.

Improved Clinch Knot How Improved Clinch Knot was connected

Its Improved Clinch Knot has been examined over time which led to an enhanced version. It's an extremely well-liked choice for those looking to attach terminal tackle to monofilament lines. The "improved" version is very popular and fishers are no longer using the traditional Clinch. This version has been improved and is swift and straightforward to tie, making it extremely solid. It is not recommended to braided lines. From the 12 best knots for fishing The Improved Clinch Knot is one of 12 excellent fishing knots, which was featured on the Pro-Knot fishing knot Cards.

Improved Clinch Knot Tying Instructions

The thread at the end of the line into the hook's eye. It will make loops when you return off the lines back towards the primary line. Utilize the tag end to create 5 or more loops around the main line. The number of turns you can make depends on the size of your line. The shorter the line, is, the more turns you'll require. After you have completed the turns, an appropriate loop is made.

Take the line's end line back. Take it through the original loop, which was in front of the eye and finally, proceed to the larger loop, which formed by dragging the tag to the beginning loop.

The knot should be wet, then draw the hook as well as the longer end. Do not drag the tag to tighten it around the coils. Then, slide it until it is snug against your eye, and it is now possible to cut the tag's end off in a way that it closes. Don't be scared to cut the tag.

The Baja Knot

How the Baja Knot Is Tied

It is the Baja Knot is a Perfection Loop and comes with an attached hook inside the loop. Loops that are utilized to make a loop on the point where lines meet is called the Perfection Loop. It's a highly efficient method for forming loop-to-loop connection and is able to be tied in a small size in the event that you require it.

It's the method by which it is done by the Mexican Panga Skippers tie their hook in knots, this is how it's executed. The term was coined to describe"Baja Knot" "Baja Knot".

This knot type is excellent and can work very well for heavy mono- if heavier than one hundred pounds leader! It's very simple to tie, and has proven to be extremely solid. Once you've learned the knot and have mastered the method, making the knot is straightforward.

When you're done making the knot it is crucial to secure the hook or lure (which can be found inside the boat or on a clamp) after which you draw the line that is standing until it is very solid in order to ensure that the knot in strong mono. After it is secured the knot should slide completely. Be aware of the place the location where the hook hangs and it is usually from the loop that is non-slip. This is an important consideration for live bait or a bait for swimming. This is due to the fact that the hook used for free-swing allows room to allow for a natural baiting behavior.

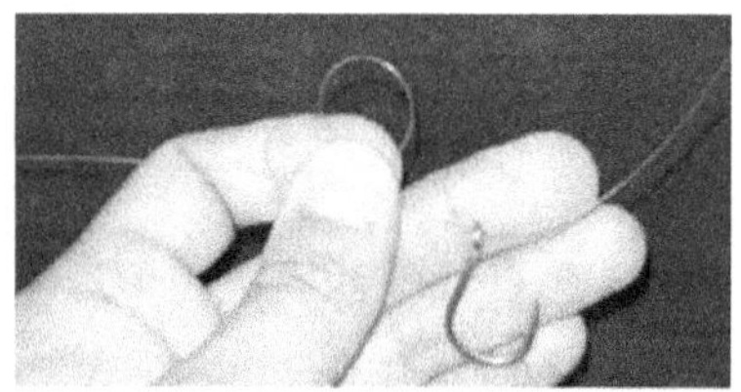

Tying Instructions for Baja Knot

The initial step is create a basic loop. The loop should be just a couple of inches off from the last on the primary line. It is the biggest one of three loops constructed from the knot. Attach a hook to the center of the loop. You must allow it to remain in place while knotting the second part of the knot.

Pick the part of the line which is in the open and place it on the outside of the first loop. after that, you can place it to the side of the line that leads to the creation that of the 2nd loop. Press between your thumb and the your forefinger and pull the to the end of the tag, so that your loop is a little smaller than the original loop.

Continue the process in this manner so that you can create the loop however, make sure that the loop is an appropriate size. Then, move the hook until you reach the very top of the loop. The hook should be positioned over the loop in the middle underneath the loop on top. Make the knot in such a way that it's slightly snug.

Attach the hook with an plier or an existing railing for boats, after which it is important to push the stand line extremely in order to pull the knot to a strong mono. The knot should not slide.

The Davy Knot

What is the procedure for tying a Davy knots are tied?

A knot called the Davy Knot is the type of knot that has been attributable to Davy Wotton; it is an English Fly-Fishing professional. One of the advantages of this knot is the fact that it has power, speed and size which are the three main qualities that a knot for fishing must possess. When you've mastered the art of knotting the knot, you will make it quickly, which will give an opportunity of returning to fishing in just a little time time.

One who is extremely cautious when it comes to knot tying may be able to notice the methods employed for tying Davy knots Davy knot are similar to the techniques used to tie the extremely secure J Knot that is used to join two lines. If you are able to learn how to apply this J Knot for tying tippet to a leader, it'll allow you to tie your fly by using this Davy Knot a cinch!

This knot is very small. knot, which is ideal for knotting small flies. The Davy knot is recommended for flies of size 18-22, and comes with a range of test rates that ranges from 85-100 percent strength of the line, which is 90% according to an safe conclusion. Each fly angler should have the Davy knot within their arsenal. If you want trying to tie it on an additional size fly it is necessary to make an additional pass required to produce"Double Davy Knot. "Double Davy Knot"

Basic Instructions for Tying the Davy Knot

Keep the hook in a straight position, then take the hook off and insert it into the eye of the hook up or 4 inches the leader or the part of the thread.

Make an overhand knot just ahead of the hook. However, you should make the knot loose.

Remove the tag and then bring it back into the loop. Make sure to pass it through the knot between the overhand and the hook. It should be possible to create a figure eight.

It is recommended to take a gentle pull on the running line as you grip the end of the tag in order to tighten the knot. it will create the knot. It will then be pulled onto the main line which creates the knot.

Simple adjustments can stop the knot in place and increase the strength. It is likely that you have noticed the end of the tag is pointing to the back and is situated in the middle of the eye. If it's in the 90-degree angle and it's believed to mean that you have seated the Davy knot is sitting properly.

Tying a Snell Knot

It's the Snell Knot was invented to use with hooks that had no eyes However, it's still being used in the modern world. Saltwater anglers employ this more often for fishing live bait, and it is very well-liked by freshwater bass anglers that turn and throw Texas equipment into matted plants The hook stays straight thanks to it while fishing for fly fish using tubes.

The use of the Snell Fishing Knot has several benefits. It is possible to use the knot to secure monofilament braids, or fluorocarbon lines. This knot remains within the line of the shank of the hook, which makes it more sturdy and more convenient when trying to find a great hook set. The fishing knot is not likely to come in loose form or easily slips off.

Snell Knot Tying Instructions

It is recommended to spend time time working on your skills and understanding how to tie a knot as Snell. Easy Snell is not that difficult. It is merely the steps below before you can tie a Snell Knot.

1. The first step is run the tag end of the line through the hook eye until it reaches the end of hook.

2. Create a tiny loop. by forming the loop, it will allow you pull the tag's end back behind the hook's shank. It is possible to leave

around 4 inches from the tag's end to allow you to manipulate the tag end.

3. Wrap the tag-end of the line over the shank of the hook; you may start from point towards the eye.

4. Keep wrapping until you've got around 5 to 7 wraps. After that, place the tag on the loop from underside and up.

5. Make sure you hold the wraps to the desired position, and take the tag off and pull it towards the remaining end until it is possible to tie the knot.

6. The tag can be cut off at the ends if you'd like.

Double Pitzin

The knot that I would want to demonstrate is the fishing in the flour cabin knot, which is a double pitzin. The most appealing thing that the double pitzin knot has is the fact that the more you pull, the tighter the knot becomes.

It is easy to demonstrate ways to secure it up on chatter bait.

First step is double the length of your line and then pass through the eye of the hook. It is possible to do it twice prior to passing it through the eye, or simply pass it through as one line, and run it in the same eye however not entirely to prevent the line from completely escaping.

After you've finished that step, you'll have an unfinished loop between the opposite side of your main line, as well as crossing over to the other side.

It is recommended to hold the main line, as well as the tagging on the index finger of your hand as well as the loop portion of the line is placed over your index finger, going towards the upward direction. It is recommended to stretch the lines so that you can create a wider loop. You then take the initial loop created and rotate it three times in the loop you constructed.

After you have been able to turn it around three times in the loop constructed, you will use the loop that was made and then pass it through the second loop which was constructed, which was tethered around three times.

The loop is then dragged along the main line. After that, pull the main line and finally, if you cut that loop, as well as the tagging. and you'll be left with the main line that is straight up to the rode.

Snail Knot

Another knot crucial for any bass fishing person to understand is called the snail knot. Making the switch to the knot that is snail will assist you in getting greater numbers of fish than if you choose a different type knot. This knot mostly utilized on hooks with stretchy heads. The knot is often used in methods like punching or flipping mats, or on really dense plants.

The most attractive thing with the knot snail is once the fish has hooked it, the slender hook clicks and then flexes in the mouth of the fish.

The hook will use braids to secure the knot onto the hook. First, use the braided line to run it through into the hook's eye, with the hook's eye facing downwards, and your line must be flowing upwards. It is then possible to take around five inches of line, and then make an elongated loop. Place the ends of the line in the loop that you have made onto the hook's shank.

This means that you will get a loop at the one side of the hook, and tags on the other side, which is located at the shank. The thing you're required to do now is use the tag you inserted into the hook's shank and wrap it around shank between six and eight times. It creates a form of wrapping around that shank.

The next step is taking the loop you made initially, and any tag leftover from the wrapping was created is passed over the loop. Then, you take the main line and pull it to make it tighter.

Be sure to pull the line carefully to ensure that you don't lose the loop. After you've finished then you will have the main line, and the tag line, and an encircling over the shank your hook. which will secure the line knotted. Cut off the tag line if want, and that will be the snail knot.

Chapter 14: The Palomar Knots

This knot is most likely one of the most favored knots used in fishing seasons. If you are talking about a knots for fishing which is attracting the interest of fishermen all over all over the world, you're talking of it being the Palomar knot.

It is very simple to tie. It is extremely strong and will withstand the rigors of extreme abuse. But, now it depends on the fishing line you braid you're using and you might think that you could increase the number knots that are overhand to ensure there is no leakage. If you continue to practice it, you'll be able to tie this knot just right and perfectly placed over the hook's eye, and it will be all set for the biggest fish of its life.

For you to be able tie the knot:

You will need to bend the line

Use the braided lines and then double it by wrapping it around to create two lines of approximately 8 to 12 inches line. Then, it helps create the loop.

It is then possible to create that loop so that it goes across the eye on the hook's swivel or whatever lure you wish to apply. The eye on the lure you're using has a small eye and you want to run the line over its eye prior to creating a loop from it. You should ensure that there are approximately 6 inches of doubled line which is not inside from the eyes of your hook.

Tie a overhand knot

Then tie an overhand knot loosely and ensure that the hook hangs from the top. The way to make an overhand knot by passing the loop of the line through both the tag and main line before passing into the hole which was made.

The bolt can be tightened when it's removed, however you must ensure it's not being separated.

Run the hook over

Make use of your fingers to tie the knot that you made before you slide the knot you made onto the hook or lure that you're using and then slide it over the eye.

Cinch and Cut the Tag End

Slowly tighten the line as well as the end of the tag at the opposite end. Once you reach the point of no return, get it wet again.

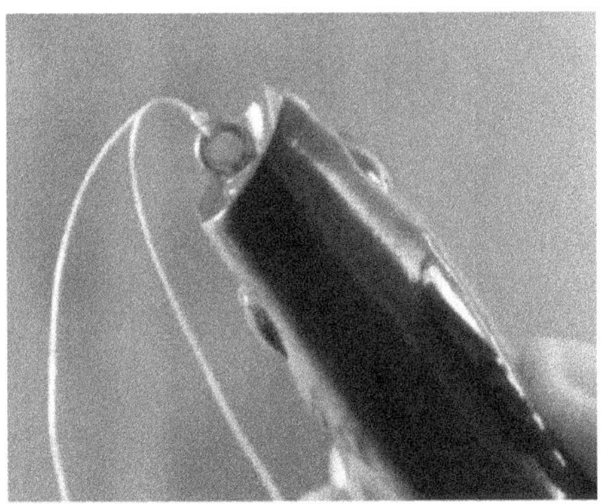

Make use of scissors or an electric clipper to trim the tag's end close to the knot.

Be sure that the various parts in the Palomar knot are securely secured after the lure hook, or any other one you're using passes through the loop. If it's not properly secured the knot could break.

If you're using braids and are fishing in a hefty structure, you might connect this knot onto the line.

The knot is sometimes referred to as it is also known as the Uni knot. It's also an elongated loop knot, this knot is commonly utilized when you want to attach a lure to tippet or lure to leaders. The knots of this type creates the loop which is located near the bottom of the line. This allows the lure or fly to to move in a fluid manner throughout the waters.

When You Should Use the Duncan Loop Knot

The Duncan knot, or The Duncan Loop Knot or Duncan Loop Knot with the monofilament, braided lines, or the fluorocarbon. It is regarded as one of the many fishing knots, which is utilized for attaching the lure or fly to the tippet of your leader. The Duncan Loop fishing knot retains much of its original breaking force, so you could make use of it to connect fishing lines to the reel's arbor as well as for connecting two lines with a similar diameter.

If you are learning the art of fishing, this knot is an excellent knot to use to learn how to tie. It is this because it is multi-purpose and easy to tie. It can be utilized for freshwater and saltwater fishing conditions.

Method of tieing an Duncan Loop Knot

Based on the knowledge you know about the times you should make use of Duncan Loop Knot Duncan Loop or the Uni Knot It's time to learn the process of tieing the knot. Take these easy steps to learn how to tie Duncan Loop Knots. Duncan Loop Knot

The line is intended to pass by the hook, or lure, based on the one you're using, and then an angle backwards parallel to the stand line, in order to create a loop created along the line. At the end of your tag, it is also there.

Take the tag's top end at the tag and wrap it around the stand line five or six times. After that, pull the line that is in the stand and the tag's end until you adjust them according so that they fit. If you are able to capsize it is possible to wrap more rounds on top of the 5 or 6 rounds wrapped around the stand line.

You may add water to the knot, and then alter the length of the loop even more by pulling on the stand line. Trim the tag's end If you want.

It's all you need to complete for tying knots such as the Duncan Loop or the Uni Knot. When you've mastered the tying process of this knot then you're able to move forward in learning to tie different knots used in fishing, as well as different types of rigs.

It is the sling knot it is possible to tie it into the ring or the lure.

Comparing the Duncan Loop Knot the Uni Knot

If you are asking yourself if there's a distinction in Duncan Loop and the Uni Knot, then you're in luck. Duncan Loop and the Uni

Knot There is a major distinction and it has the same name as an the case of. Duncan Loop or the Duncan Loop is also known as Duncan Knot was first called the Duncan Knot following Norman Duncan; he is responsible for the creation of this fishing knot in the 1960s in the beginning. However, Vic Dunaway is a ex-editor at The Miami Herald, is known for introducing this knot in the form of The Uni Knot in a fishing book written by him in the year 1970.

Bowline

The famous Alberto knot, also known as the Alberto knot or the Alberto prefer to call it, is a great line-to-line fishing knot. It's designed to join various lines with different dimensions and/or different types to braid lines. Here's the description that "Crazy Alberto" Alberto Knie described his knot as: "he said that since the very beginning of super lines, there's no true mono braided lines knots for fishing. An excellent knot is one that's one that is properly knotted.

*You would possess the braided lines and the fluorocarbon line, on two hands. Make an elongated loop with the mono leader that includes the fluorocarbon line, and making use of the braided line to go through the loop constructed for around 6-8 inches.

Add just a bit of water to it, which will help the knot come together better. Then, hold both the loop and braid line with your left hand. Once you start wrapping the braid in the two lines of mono that you have created when you make the loop. You can weave it around for eight times.

You are able to apply the same amount of water to it with your mouth before wrapping it around in the same amount of time as you did before, making each wrap over the earlier wraps constructed.

Note the loop which was made when we began so make sure you insert the tag's end back into the loop. Then, exit where it was when you first was when it entered the loop.

Pull wraps slowly until they are tight. pull it up to the top of the loop. Then, apply another coat of water with your mouth. It is not a good idea to form a mass on either side. If it is clumping over one others, you can just water it and then adjust the tension as you tug it.

Cut the tag ends of the braided line as well as the mono loop. You should aim to cut the loop as close as possible to the edge.

It is a knot that is very simple to tie. It is an excellent knot.

The FG knot can be quite difficult to tie. One of the most common complaint against knots tied with the FG knot, is that it takes way too time to tie. It's a thin knot, which is why you'll be completely in agreement to that point if you tie it using the old fashion method that is by wrapping the and tying it in the middle of the mono.

Although, it seems complicated, however there's an easier and quicker method to tie the FG knot. When you've mastered the knot, you will be capable of tying it in just 60 minutes.

Then let's go through the steps of tie knots for the FG knot.

1. Step 1: You must take the line, and wrap it around with your pinky finger, or keep it between your teeth.

This gives you a chance to put tension in the line, while you have nine fingers for making the knot. This will ensure that the line isn't moving.

Step 2: wrap the leader around the braid.

The leader should be placed on top of the braid. Begin wrapping it around the braid. Ensure that the tension remains maintained on the line to prevent it from sliding. After you have finished wrapping the braid, you can now create another wrap underneath the braid. It is done through wrapping around the braid in a continuous manner until you've got around 16 wraps per individual; this could be about 22 wraps.

3. The knot should be secured, therefore, it is recommended to tie two half-hitch knot so that the coil is secured.

Make sure to hold the coils you have created using your fingers in order to hold the coils in place. Also, make sure you're putting both the mainline and leader within these knots to be over the coils.

4. Tension is to be applied to knots to allow the braid to penetrate the leader.

This knot type is most effective if the braid is able to dig into the leader. So, once you've put the coils into place Then, put the braid in your hands a few times before pulling on the knot in order to allow it to sink.

As you continue pulling at the lines, you'll notice that every one of the coils are becoming more secure on the braid, and are equally spaced.

The first one is the one that's most crucial of the others and, therefore, you need make sure it has been tightened. If it isn't, you be at risk of this knot becoming loose in particular if it's an ax you're casting into.

Step 5: will cut the top of the tag on the leader

You can cut off the tag's end and bring it back to the knot once it's secured and it will not move.

But, ensure that you cut the tag's end off after you make sure that you have tensioned the knot.

As you put a strain around your knot, coils gradually move up but you're not advised to remove the tag's ends prior to that.

6. You need to tie a minimum of two half-hitch knots

The reason this step was made is to allow the top edge of the knot more smooth in order that the rough edge of the tag doesn't catch on something, be it floated debris, rod guides or whichever it may be.

Chapter 15: Standard Bowline Knot

The type of knot described above is one that makes an unbreakable loop placed at the very end of a rope line. It's a straightforward knot to tie, and it is possible to remove it very easily, which is why it's very effective for various circumstances. It's extremely popular, and is utilized for carrying heavy loads and this is why it's extremely popular for boating. Sometimes, it is referred to as"the king of knots" in the event that you tie a bowline, make sure that it is not prone to slippage and jamming.

Between other things among other uses, the among other things, one thing you can be assured of is it could be utilized whenever you want to be climbing. It can be used for an emergency rescue or transport a load. Make sure to use the stopper knot in order to make sure it's secured particularly if you use it for a climb. But, we do not advise that you lean too heavily upon a bowline knot during diverse climbing conditions, since it's a knot that is easy to loosen.

How to Tie the Standard Bowline Knot:

Then you'll create a loop using the working line over the regular line.

Then, the other part of the line runs through the loop you made from the bottom.

You wrap the other end of the rope over the remaining portion of the rope, and then band your working end of the rope you wrapped around the stand end, and then pass it through the loop. The origin of the rope is unclear.

After that, take the working portion of the rope. Hold the end that is standing on the rope, pulling it tight to secure the knot. The knot is now complete.

Due to the nature of actions performed with the knot of bowline, it is recommended to take all precautionary steps to ensure that one doesn't be a victim of regrets.

In most instances, this knot is utilized for climbing, and is an extremely impactful exercise and comes with many risks associated with climbing. It is therefore essential to be prepared, practice with direction, and adhere to the extensive safety guidelines that are offered when trying to climb.

There are some possible disadvantages to the bowline knot. If you are rock climbing make sure that you know that the knot in a bowl isn't suitable for climbing. The knot isn't ideal for caving as it is very easy to loosen the tie. When the bowline bears loads, it may be difficult to take it off.

Below are some of the numerous situations in which you could use a bowine knot.

Boating:

This knot is usually employed to bind the mooring line on the boat to an object that is solid and in an appropriate location, such as the post, tree or anchor. It is used for tying lines together in sailing and boating expeditions.

Rescue missions:

If someone is trying to save someone else, they typically utilize a rope for tying to the victim, but the knot wouldn't be as tight, and ought to be simple to tie. This is when the bowline knot is used.

Tying Hammocks:

The knot is typically utilized to tie the hammock to two stakes or trees. It could also be utilized to attach the handle line to the kite.

Horses:

The horse owners use bowline knots for tying their horses to a post for hitching.

Double Bowline or water Bowline knot

It is known as the Double Bowline can also be called the Round-Turn Bowline and sometimes most people misunderstand it as an Water Bowline. It's a standard Bowline Knot and it has Double Overhand Loops or just an arcing turn around the Bight. This is a great option for those who want to participate with rough terrain which is the reason it is necessary to boost the force and durability in this Double Bowline and can be employed for rigging that is heavy-duty.

If you examine the knot's tittle it will be clear how ambiguous it could be. This is because it is not destined to turn out as an actual Bowline that has two loops particularly when you consider it in relation to the Spanish Bowline or the French Bowline.

Instructions for Tying Double Bowline Knot

First step is create two loops by wrapping the rope on your left hand and using the free end hanging down. Repeat the process to create another loop, which is less than the previous loop.

Start with the first loop, and then place it over the other loop. Take the working end and then pass it through both loops that are at to the beginning to the bottom. After that, wrap the line around one time, then take it through the 2 loops you constructed. Check to see if there's an existing loop kept because it is the loop you will use to tie to anything. If you're done to tie the knot by pulling on the free end as you are keeping the line on a stand.

Running Bowling Knot

The knots of this kind tend to create a knot or the appearance of a sliding loop. It is extremely useful in situations where one wants to retrieve the object. You can throw the loop in the open area around the object. it will serve to secure the object while you pull the line tightly. The knot does not bind to the line that is in place, therefore it is able to be easily lost or removed.

The Instructions for Tying Running Bowline Knot

Double line the rope and make sure you cross the work end of the rope, as the running bowling will occur in the center part of the loop.

Make a loop that's tiny on top of the first loop you made. The method is to create an arc of the line across the line.

Remove the tag's end that is removed from the working end, and place it in the loop you have created earlier.

Pull the tag through, and then from below it is wrapped at the ends once more around the top side of the larger loop, which was initially made then pull it back into the second loop that was created, by the small loop.

Then, pull the tag as well as the other part of the big loop in order to tighten the knot. When you tie this knot you will be able to pull the opposite side of the rope to hold an object in your hand and then tighten the knot.

This is the place to connect a bowline. It must be placed at the center of the Bight. It creates a secure loop in the middle of the line. It's most commonly utilized when you wish to create two loops at the loop at the top of the line. It can also be used as an un-slip loop, but the free end isn't useful. It can be used as a knot for a sling or a knot, to serve as a bosum's seat in a emergency rescue situations that are an emergency. The two loops are able to be fashioned into various dimensions if needed.

How do you tie the bowline onto the Bight

You can make a double-section of line that automatically creates a loop. Then create a loop, or "eye" within this double line. Then you'd create a loop automatically to the opposite side.

Place the newly generated loop underneath the loop, which will form the double loop. Then, push it through the loop that is above it, before using the loop you put across the loop before to pass with the entire rope in reverse.

Now you can tie the knot by pulling the double loop as you're holding the line in a standing position.

Figure 8 Knot in Bight

The knot of this type is typically used to secure a bight on the middle of the rope. It is typically employed for "tie-in" onto the rope. Tieing a figure-eight knot in a bight can be one of the largest knots and it is characterized by gradual curves when compared to knots that are overhand, it's easily identified through the distinctive "8" form. The knot is much safer over the knot bowline.

Applications

The knot can be tied to the rope for securement of a rescuer, litters, anchor plates, anchorages or any other piece of equipment that is attached to the end of rope.

Directions

Form two lines. an arc that crosses the edges of the rope. Then, wrap the rope around the second part of the rope. This will form the loop.

Then, take the bight back to where it came from. This time it needs to be above and not below. Put the bight in place into the loop you made and then pull it back to close it.

Be sure that the lines which run below the loop are straight and properly dressed.

The majority of people tie security knots on the opposite side of the line to serve protection reasons.

Figure 8 Knot Tied In the End

Then, you'll have to pull through the fixed ring to aid you to tie an eight figure.

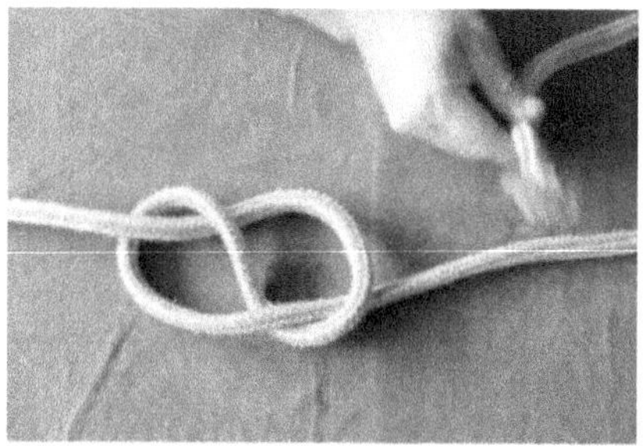

The first step is tie a straightforward figure eight in the center of your rope. You can then use the working part of the rope through the ring you intend to use. You should then determine the direction coincides with the figure 8 that you connected.

Once you have passed your rope through the ring, take the working end which has put through the ring and into an arc of figure 8 knot was knotted. It will form a loop that runs towards the rings.

Continue to trace the route of the figure eight you designed before. Then, shift the working end of the rope in the similar steps as if need to tie a figure eight. The rope should be to run parallel to one others and to move the rope around. You then cinch it to make it tighter. If you'd like more protection then you could tie an overhand stopper knot just above the figure 8 knot.

The majority of mountain climbers are blessed with a solution, that is the figure eight knot and the double knot over hand.

Chapter 16: Basic Boating Knots

It is important to learn how knots are tied to ensure that they are effective in their application.

Clove Hitch Knot

How you are to tie the Clove Hitch;

An easy clove knot is a knot that can be used for any purpose. It's easy to tie and untie. The Clove Hitch is a practical and easy to tie knot. Clove Hitch makes a excellent knot to tie. As a hitch, it should use with care, as it is possible for it to slide off or become untied when the item it's tied to is inclined to turn or move, or if continuous pressure is not kept in the string.

Tying Instructions for Clove Hitch Knot

Place the rope you intend to use on the post.

Wrap the rope around the post, then around the post once more.

Slide the working end of the rope underneath the last wrap made at the top of the pole.

Then pull it in both directions to make it tighter.

If you're not happy with how your lock works, you may include an additional lock it, or even add an overhand knot.

Timber Hitch

How you can tie the Timber Hitch Knot;

It can be used to secure the rope around the post or any other circular object. It is not jammed and does not slide no matter what the weight of the load and is easy to tie and simple to remove. It is suggested to finish the Timber Hitch by using either one or two half hitches that are close to the end that is hauling in order to prevent the weight from bending.

The Timber Hitch Knot Tying Instructions

1. Put the work end of the rope you intend to utilize around the object, then rotate it to the pole you're using towards us.

2. Put the end that is working of the rope you turned to rotate the pole into the small lop which is created after you attempted to slip your rope across the pole.

3. After that, you should pass the at the working end of the rope through the loop around three times, using the length of the rope.

4. There is the option of adding the half hitches just close to the hauling point to allow hoisting to prevent the your load from twisting.

How to Tie the Alpine Butterfly Knot

The ALPINE BUTTERFLY KNOT It is referred to by different names. The Butterfly Knot is due to the shape it adopts as you tie to form a sturdy loop that is located in the center of your rope. It can be used to carry loads from any direction, and also together.

It's also helpful when you are making an un-slip loop through between the two ropes, so that carabiners can be attached, which can provide places of attachment for other lines to be joined, and for example, the Alpine Butterfly is very useful for rescue operations using a canoe. It can also be utilized to figure the part of a rope has been damaged.

Instructions for knotting an Alpine Butterfly Knot

The rope should be used to weave a loop into the rope. Then twist the rope as if you were going to connect the rope.

Twist it in a complete rotation to create an eight-shaped shape.

The top edge of the eight downwards to the lowest point of eight.

Now you can take it out of the lower opening of the knot with an eight shape and then pull it in tight.

Sheepshank Knot

How to tie the Sheepshank Knot;

The knot, in actuality, should not be used in all cases and is best avoided. It's often utilized in order to cut a rope shorter, but it's not a secure knot, and may break fast if there's an interruption in tension to the knot, particularly for synthetic rope. If you've got a damaged part of your rope it could be isolated making use of the

Sheepshank knot. You will need to keep tension to the knot. It is possible to use the Alpine Butterfly Knot to substitute for the role of rope isolation and rope shortening and is one knot you can depend on.

Sheepshank Knot Tying Instructions

Starting from the rope you wish to reduce create the loop.

Make two additional loops with that same rope.

Continue to pass the bight from this second loop by one loop before proceeding to in the final loop.

You can then pull free ropes of the middle loop to insert into the rope that was already in the third rope as you pull the second loops in opposing directions.

Be sure to keep the knot in a tight position.

Blood Knots

The majority of fly fishermen utilize blood knots. This technique is employed for when you need to join two lines for fishing with identical lengths. It is not easy to tie but it generally takes time to learn. First step is begin learning to tie two strings in order to master the fundamental blood knot. When you are confident with your technique of tie your knot, then you can practice tying your next trip to fly fish! Blood knots are one of the most commonly used knot for fishing.

How do I secure the knot of blood

It is suggested to place the two lines on a floor that is smooth, and then assign them labels, you can use lines A and B for their labels.

Choose the two lengths of string, or the fishing line and put them in a way that they will be placed next to one another.

Make sure that two pieces aren't too separated, but are near each other, so it is easy to knot the two pieces. In order to make it simple for knotting, be sure to mark the string that is left as line A. Then, label that to the right of the string is thought as line B.

If you're using the fishing line to learn the knot, it could be easy to practice knotting this knot with your shoelaces, or chunks of yarn. Keep working on it until you're skilled in knotting it.

Make a small loop that has both lengths joined It should be loose and not very tight.

Start by weaving the two strings around one another, and then use the black rope to wrap onto the blue rope depending on the colour of rope that you intend to utilize and doesn't limit you from using the particular kind of rope. It is recommended to let untied ends hang from the string's longer length or on the fishing line. Be sure to ensure that the piece of string that you've recently made form a fundamental twist rather than creating knots.

The lengths of string which were created should appear similar to an pretzel.Take line A, tie it to the opposite side of line B, which is the left side. Wrap five times. Continue twisting line A around B. This makes a shape which can be wrapped around the second length of string. This sting needs to move to move counterclockwise. This will create a circle around line A line B at least of five times.

You must ensure that you are holding your hand firmly at the top of line A. This makes the string less likely unwind.

Find the line's ending A and place it in the space between line A and B. Make use of the ending of line A is currently in your hands and then pull it towards the left. Create a curved strings over the coils and ensure that it's aligned between lines A and B. Keep pulling your string downwards leaving at the least one inch, that's roughly 2.5 cm of slack. This originates beginning on line A.

Don't be concerned even if your string isn't too tight. Allow the string to remain in position, which will cause the initial part of the knot unwind.

The end of the string will rest over the portion of string that has been coiled.

Create a curly curl by with line B that will turn around the other side of line A five times. Make use of the line B which is loose, and begin to create a circle going clockwise around the straight length of line A. Create a loop which can be shaped to wrap around the line A. Do the loop in a circular manner and this creates the exact coil shape has been formed at the end of the knot. Make a circular motion about for at least 5 times. That is the case if you want the blood knot to be extremely robust; in this case the case, make a circle around the string for between 10 and 14 times.

Be sure to ensure that your coils in line across the two sides of the knot you're making. If you're looping Line A around line B seven times, then you need to repeat the process for line B on the other side in the blood knot.

Take one end of the line B between lines A and B. It is important to ensure that you tie this section of your blood knot on the opposite direction, and by making sure the end that is loose from line B is securely secured. Then, take the end of line B and place it underneath the coil. Then tug it. It should be pulled up and down between lines B and A. In the same manner as you pulled the other side, ensure that you verify that it exceeds one-inch of slack in the gap, that is 2.5 millimeters.

It is important to ensure that the edges of the knot which is loose are facing in opposite directions.

There are two ends that have been left loose that need to be pulled away from the two lines that is lines A and B. Make use of your hands to grasp the two loose ends from the knot. You must use the same amount of pressure to pull on both ends in order that they tighten the knot and secure it. Look closely; you'll see that the knot is becoming small. If the knot was tied didn't turn out as well in your initial tests, don't be concerned. All you have to do is continue to try to make it better. You should concentrate on winding and then tucking into the string.

Check that your knot is taut and there shouldn't be any strings that are loose that are not present.

There may be some untidy slacks left from the lines. You can remove them. Make use of scissors to cut or cut off nearly every single piece of string. Make sure to cut off the entire length of it. If you don't it is, you'll have to undo the knot completely. Instead, leave room we have some slack that is usable and easily visible.

If you'd prefer less slack remains visible and visible, simply remove half of the extra.

Make sure to check the lines you can be certain you are tied securely. Make use of your two hands to ensure that you hold the length larger than the length of string you have just tied with the other. Give both ends one good tug. If both strings stay in place, you be able to tie an artery knot!

Chapter 17: Understanding Knots

Knots are an essential part of the human experience. Whether you're tying a boat to a dock, using it to make a hammock, or even creating your unique knot, knots can do so much more than just keep your hair out of your face. But there are so many different kinds of knots! Some have simple, elegant closures, whereas others have intricate designs or special materials to create a more secure connection. Knots can be used for everyday tasks (like tying shoes), or they can be used for more elaborate purposes like building bridges and buildings.

Understanding knots is fundamental to any type of work that involves rope or other forms of rope-like material. For example, not every knotted cord is good for tying. A signature knot used by the military and engineering communities is known as the Airman's Loop, which doesn't serve any specific purpose but looks cool! The Airman's Loop is probably one of the most famous knots in the world. Although not all types of knots are important, having a firm understanding of knots is essential to everything from tying up boxes and furniture to securing ropes and cargo on boats. Depending on the type you tie, the finished knot can be secure, simple-looking, or extremely complex.

Knots have been used in countless applications since the beginning of time. Some of the earliest evidence for human knot usage dates back to about 10,000 BC, when flax fiber cords were used in various ways by a prehistoric person. Ceramic statues dating back to 7000–5000 BC include carvings that depict men tying knots with rope-like material. There is evidence that these knots were used in crafts, cordage, and other products dating back to 14,000 BC. Knots have been one of the most important pieces of rope technology throughout time; however, recent developments in engineering have made the use of knots less common.

Different types of knots are used for different purposes. There are many different kinds of knots that allow people to create unique and complex-looking closures that not everyone can master! Some types of knots are used all the time; however, others make up a special niche in rope applicability. Some knots are used for special types of ascetics, and others have a unique purpose.

One of the most common knots is the overhand knot, typically used to start and finish a piece of rope. Remember that an overhand knot always forms a loop. An overhand knot can be used to tie shoes, close bags, or any other type of cordage structure. Other knots are useful for symbolic purposes: like the Carrick Bend (named after James Carrick), which is often used when creating jewelry like rings or bracelets. Although there are many ways to tie a Carrick Bend, it's traditionally made by interlocking two long pieces of rope into an X-shaped structure. The result is a single loop that starts at one point and tapers to the opposite point. To make a Carrick Bend, interlock the two pieces of rope together in an X pattern.

Knots can be used for so many different types of applications; however, knot usage can also be limited by the amount and type of materials available to use. In short, it depends on what you're tying and how you'll use the finished product. For example, some knots are more useful when using natural materials like hemp cordage, whereas others are easier to tie when using synthetic ropes or an electric drill! All knots can be undone with some effort (like most Marine Corps knots). This allows the use of knots in many circumstances; however, some are much more complicated or secure. For example, the Palomar knot is useful for making ropes that require an incredibly secure connection. This knot closes by tying a bight to a start and overhand loop at the rope's end until it is completely tied off. The Palomar knot has many different variations, including Tightening (a process used to close this type of knot) and Wrestling (used to tighten this type of knot).

Though most knots are pretty straightforward, some require special techniques or materials to be used effectively. One of the most common and oldest knots is the Bowline, a quick and easy way to tie a loop at the end of a piece of rope. Instead of creating an overhand or underhanded loop, you create an overhand loop and tie it off with another overhand knot. Another knot that is used to secure items in bulk is known as the Fisherman's knot. This type of knot relies on each rope end having one half hitched around the other before being pulled tightly to secure them together. All fishermen should know how to tie the fisherman's knot!

Knots can be used for so many different things because they are designed for specific purposes. I think it's important to know the basics of knots and how they are used. Not knowing the right knot for a certain application could be embarrassing and lead to a bad experience! You don't want to cover your face in snotty nose-wrinkles because you weren't aware that snot can be tied to an overhand loop or that there are different types of knots depending on the type of rope used.

Knowing the right knots can save you from a world of suffering!

Chapter 18: Different Types Of Hitch Knots

The Klemheist Knot

The Klemheist Knot is tied by making a Prusik Loop with a cord or rope that is no more than 1/2 the diameter of the main, static rope. The friction loop is able to slide up the rope easily, but it will grip the rope when it is subjected to load. The knot will also slide down the rope by pushing the knot without any load on it

How to make the Knot:

Place a loop consisting of a cord that is no more than 1/2 the diameter of the main line behind the static line.

1.Wrap your line around the static line making the loop on the right side.

2.Repeat step 1, two more times working your way from the bottom to the top.

3.Feed the the loop in the left hand through loop on your right.

4.Pull left loop over to the left side of the static line and pull hard to tighten the knot.

5.Grasp the knot as a whole and slide it up the static line. Secure the knot to the static line with weight to the loop.

The Bowline Knot

The Bowline is often referred to as "The Rescue knot." This knot creates a loop at the end of your cordage, which cannot shrink or expand. In "The Scouts", this knot is often taught using the story of the rabbit coming out of its hole, in front of the tree, then going behind the tree, and back down his original hole.

The scout's rhyme: Make a loop with the top towards you. The rabbit goes out of the hole, then around the tree, and back into the hole.

How to make the Knot:

1.Form a loop on top of the line's long end, leaving enough cord for your desired loop size.

2.Just like when you are making an overhand knot, pull the free end of the rope through your loop. Continue around behind the line and then back through the small loop.

3.While maintaining the secondary loop that will become your Bowline loop, bring down the free end from the original loop.

The Figure-Eight Knot

The Figure-Eight Knot is a more secure knot than most knots; it can be used for preventing cords and ropes from fraying and as a stopper. Rock climbers use it often for tying Caribinas (strong metal snap clips) onto ropes, and it is a favorite for securing overhead weights

How to make the Knot:

1.Tie a single eight in your cord, two feet from its end.

2.Pass the free end through any secure tie-in point if desired.

3.Retrace the original eight with the free end, leaving a loop at the bottom of the size you require.

4.Pull all four strands of cord to cinch down the knot.

The Water (Tape) Knot

A water knot or tape knot can tie two ropes together or to two tape ends. When it's used with the tape, it's usually called a tape knot. It is mostly used to make a sling or a runner.

How to make the Knot:

1.It would help if you created an overhand knot – this beginning is the same for the tape and the rope. If you're making a tape knot, just bend the tape in the same direction.

2.With the next tape or knot, do the same as with the first one, only backward through the knot.

3.When pulling the rope, make sure it goes evenly around the rope or the tape.

The Strangle Knot

Strangle knot is a Binding or Double Overhand knot great for keeping multiple objects together with a rope that goes at least once around the objects, and it can secure the neck of a sack. It is also quite similar to a constrictor knot, but the main difference between them is that Strangle knot's ends go at the outside edges, and with the constrictor knot, they go between the turns.

How to make the Knot:

1.Go with the rope around the bar and then cross it with the first turn.

2.Pass the rope again, going in the same direction.

3.Tuck, the rope under the first, turns and makes sure to tighten them strong enough.

The Alpine Butterfly Bend

Alpine butterfly bend is a very reliable and common bend derived from the better-known Alpine Butterfly Loop. It's easy to tie and untie even after being loaded. Climbers often use it to join two ropes, even if temporarily, and it's very similar to the Zeppelin and Hunter's loop in that it's interlocking knots overhand. However, its advantage is that it is easily untied with fingers, while the knots mentioned above would have to be cut to be released.

Besides its strength and reliability, we believe its fame also comes from being connected and similar to the Alpine Butterfly Loop – where if you learn one, you're halfway through making the other.

How To make the Alpine Butterfly bend:

1. Take two ends and join them

2. Wrap the rope around your hand

3. With the joint on the fingertips, go around once more

4. Bend the joint back and under the ropes

5. Slide the knot off your hands and tighten it

The Slip Knot

The Slip knot is used in various situations. For climbers, a Slip knot can be used for tying gear to an anchor or few items attached to it, but it does not secure the anchor itself, so it is required to assure that the items are properly attached.

It is very practical because it can be tied with only one hand and can be made while climbing. The Slip knot is one of the most commonly used knots, and it is almost identical to the Noose Knot with the exception that the bight inserted is shaped from the short end and not the long one. It is also used in knitting but only by name as it is almost always structured as a noose.

Interestingly, the Slip Knot is sometimes used as a temporary stopper knot, as it may be used to lock the short end. It's easily untied by pulling one end or tightened around an item if attached to it.

How To make the Slip Knot:

1.Fold a loop to double it.

2.Once you have started, you can easily decide which end of the rope will actually tighten and which end will untie the Slip Knot.

3.If you are making the Slip knot where you want the right end of the rope to slip, pull the right loop through the left one, and if you want the left end to slip, you can send the left loop through the right one.

To be sure it is tightened firmly, straighten it by hand and evenly around the loop.

The Bachmann Knot

The Bachmann knot is a friction hitch that requires the use of a round cross-section carabiner. Arborists or hikers mostly use it. The knot finds the best use when the friction hitch needs to be constantly or quickly altered, but it's also easily made self-tending, so we can say it's multi-practical. The hitch is easily released by grabbing the carabiner while unloading it, sliding, and moving up or down when needed.

The best is to use the locking carabiner for the Bachmann knot since you will be taking it to move the hitch. Moving the hitch is done by unclipping the top loop and releasing the cord. If you are using a non-locking carabiner, to make sure the knot is safe

, it is best to use it with the carabiner gate opened facing down. That way, it will have much less chance of unclipping itself.

How To make the Bachmann Knot:

1.Make a band of rope or simply use a pre-made tie and put it into the carabiner.

2.Take the strop, wrap it around the rope while holding the carabiner against the rope, and then pull the strop through the carabiner.

3.Repeat the action once more if there is a space in the carabiner.

4.Put the load at the bottom of the strop, so the knot is in point of friction.

The Poacher's Knot

A Poacher's knot (also known as a variation of Double Overhand knot) is a very secure knot that can be used to create the foot loop to a carabiner, or cavers can use it in making a cow tail. It is a very safe hitch knot. Poacher's knot can be made out of horsehair though it is hard to imagine using that material nowadays.

How To make the Poacher's knot:

1.Start by creating a bight at the bottom of the rope.

2.Not so tight, wrap its end around that bight two times.

3.Complete the Poacher's knot by pulling its end through those turns.

www.ingramcontent.com/pod-product-compliance
Lightning Source LLC
Chambersburg PA
CBHW071620030726
47598CB00001B/368